UPTOWN–DOWNTOWN HORSECARS–TROLLEY CARS

Urban Transportation in Kingston, New York

1866–1930

Also by Glendon L. Moffett

*The Old Skilly Pot and Other Ferryboats
of Rondout, Kingston and Rhinecliff*

*To Poughkeepsie and Back:
The Story of the Poughkeepsie-Highland Ferry*

*Down to the River by Trolley:
The History of the New Paltz-Highland Trolley Line*

UPTOWN--DOWNTOWN HORSECARS--TROLLEY CARS

Urban Transportation in Kingston, New York

1866--1930

by
Glendon L. Moffett

PURPLE MOUNTAIN PRESS
Fleischmanns, New York

Uptown----Downtown; Horsecars----Trolley Cars:
Urban Transportation in Kingston, New York, 1866-1930

First edition, 1997
Published by
PURPLE MOUNTAIN PRESS, LTD.
Main Street, P.O. Box E3
Fleischmanns, New York 12430-0378
914-254-4062
914-254-4476 (fax)
Purple@catskill.net

Copyright © 1997 by Glendon L. Moffett
All rights reserved under International and Pan-American Copyright Conventions. No part of this book may be reproduced or transmitted by any means without permission in writing from the publisher.

Library of Congress Cataloging in Publication Data

Moffett, Glendon L. (Glendon Lloyd), 1931-
    Uptown--downtown, horsecars--trolley cars : urban transportation in Kingston, New York, 1866-1930 / by Glendon L. Moffett. -- 1st ed.
       p. cm.
    Includes bibliographical references (p. -) and index.
    ISBN 0-935796-91-6 (pbk. : acid-free paper)
    1. Street-railroads--New York (State)--Kingston Region--History.
I. Title.
TF725.K56M64   1997
                                         97-31881
                                              CIP

5 4 3 2 1
Manufactured in the United States of America on acid-free paper.
Cover photo: "All aboard for Rondout!" From DeLisser, *Picturesque Ulster*. Back cover photo: Courtesy The Trolley Museum of New York.

Table of Contents

Introduction — 7

Kingston and Rondout Horse Railroad Company — 9

Kingston's Great Trolley Fight: Kingston City Electric Railway vs. Colonial City Railroad — 31

Kingston Consolidated Railroad Company — 70

Appendices — 109

Bibliography — 148

Acknowledgments — 148

Index — 149

Introduction

THIS BOOK IS THE STORY OF PUBLIC TRANSPORTATION IN Rondout and Kingston, New York, during the period 1866-1930. By 1866, Rondout was a thriving port on the Hudson River. Steamers traveled daily between the port and New York City providing transportation of passengers and goods.

Many of the people who serviced this industry lived in Ponckhockie, Rondout and Kingston, and created a demand for reliable public transportation. Before 1866, they either walked, rode horses, drove carriages or used an omnibus. As technology advanced, the horse car, which rode on tracks and could carry more passengers, replaced the omnibus. Around 1893, the electric trolley replaced the horse car. There were several advantages to this new mode: A trolley did not require feeding and stabling; it did not get tired; it could run 24 hours a day.

Late in 1892, the Kingston City Electric Railroad bought the Kingston and Rondout Horse Railroad Company. This purchase gave the electric railroad a right-of-way for its track and, more importantly, the franchise to operate a line. Shortly after the announcement that the line would be electrified, a group of capitalists from New York City formed the Colonial City Electric Railway

Uptown—Downtown; Horsecars—Trolley Cars

Company. This new company planned to operate a rival line parallel to the Kingston City Electric Railroad. Hometown entrepreneur Samuel B. Coykendall of the Kingston group informed his city's common council that his own company did not object to the new line, but he warned that an impediment to the competitor's plan was the lack of a grade-level right-of-way across the West Shore Railroad tracks. Indeed, this problem plagued the Colonial City Electric Railway Company for many years.

The Kingston City Electric Railroad Company had no problem crossing the West Shore tracks at grade, since its newly acquired tracks were in place before the arrival of the West Shore line. When its competitor wanted to obtain permission to cross the railroad's tracks, the West Shore said no. After several years before the courts, the Public Service Commission and the Kingston Common Council, the management of the Colonial City Traction Company (the sucessor to the Colonial City Electric Railroad Company) was allowed to construct a tunnel under the West Shore tracks.

Another problem concerned the Strand near Rondout Creek, where the Ulster & Delaware Railroad had constructed a crossover through the Colonial City line. Employees of the two groups put in and removed this disputed crossover several times.

Eventually, New York City capitalists acquired both electric railroad lines and combined them into the Kingston Consolidated Railroad Company.

From 1866 to 1910, the public relied on horse cars and then trolley cars to provide basic urban transportation. Around 1910, Henry Ford started mass-producing cars. From then on, trolley companies fought a losing battle against the freedom of travel offered by the automobile. To remain in business, the company would ask for periodic fare increases or would propose abandoning parts of the system. By 1930, buses had replaced all of Kingston's picturesque trolleys.

The Kingston and Rondout Horse Railroad Company

IN SEPTEMBER 1863, A GROUP OF MEN FROM KINGSTON AND Rondout began talking about replacing their communities' omnibus system with a horse railroad between Rondout Creek and Esopus Creek. An omnibus was a wagon, roofed to protect passengers from inclement weather and enclosed on three sides, with doors at the rear. It was pulled by one or two horses. Passengers sat on benches along both sides and at the end of the omnibus nearest the driver. It was difficult to enter and leave the frequently odoriferous omnibus due to low headroom and usually crowded conditions.

At that time, omnibuses, which could carry only a limited number of passengers, traveled mainly over dirt roads. The combination of narrow wheels, heavy loads and rain often resulted in stuck vehicles. To overcome these limitations, other cities had introduced horse-car railroads. Metal rails on which these cars rode greatly reduced friction and allowed more passengers to be pulled using the same horsepower. Also, a horse car could be pulled faster than an omnibus. This resulted in a lower passenger-per-mile operating cost. The horse railroad had one drawback though: It could go only where the rails went. However, the advantages far outweighed this.

UPTOWN—DOWNTOWN; HORSECARS—TROLLEY CARS

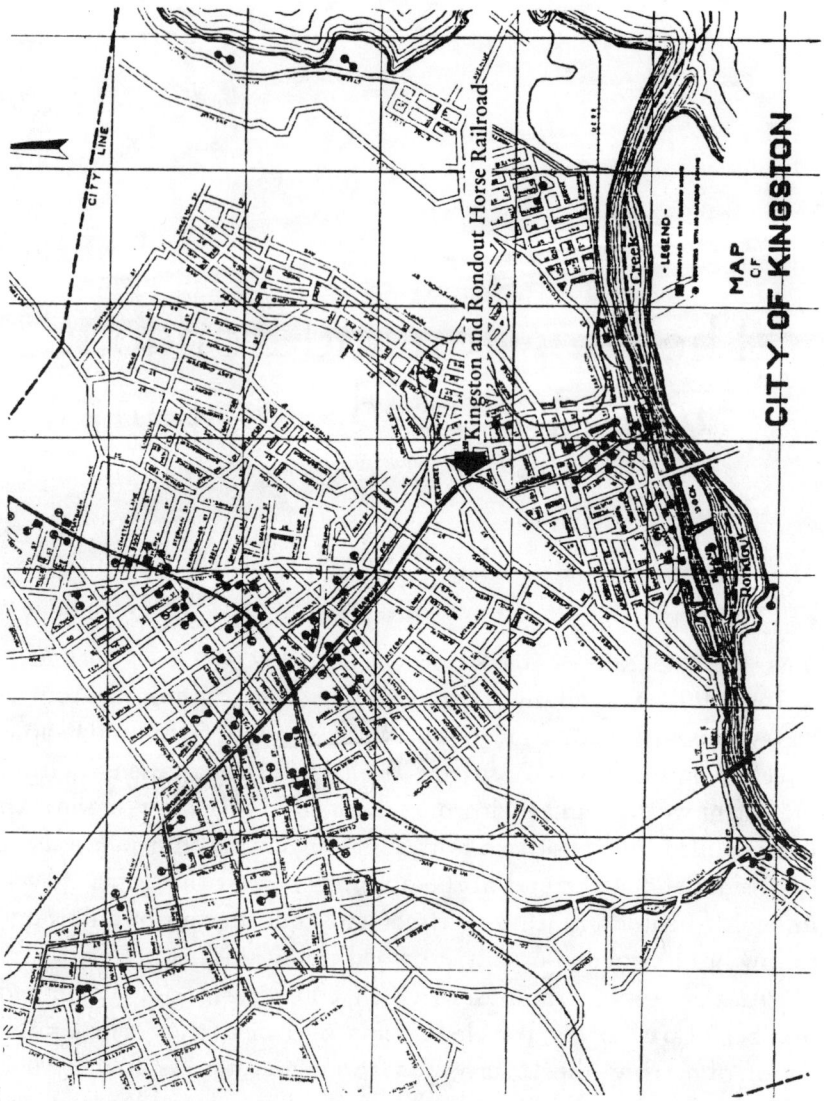

Above: Map of Kingston and Rondout Horse Railroad.
Courtesy The Trolley Museum of New York (map modified by the author)

Opposite page top: Omnibus on Lower Broadway.
Bottom: Horsecar #1 on Lower Broadway.
Both courtesy Eugene Dauner

Urban Transportation in Kingston, New York, 1866-1930

Uptown—Downtown; Horsecars—Trolley Cars

In February 1864, the businessmen submitted a proposal to the New York State Legislature to form the Kingston and Rondout Railroad Corporation. The incorporators said that the construction of their road would begin once they received approval and the weather warmed up. By October, the founders signed the Articles of Association and appointed 13 directors, including Thomas Cornell, Henry D. H. Snyder, Jonathan H. Hasbrouck, Elias T. Van Nostrand, Lewis N. Hermance, Henry A. Samson, Lorenzo A. Sykes, Robert Atwater, William C. More, Michael J. Madden, Jansen Hasbrouck, Elihu J. Baldwin and William H. Wells. (See Appendix A for a list of trustees in other years.) The capital stock for the company was fixed at $125,000 with each of the 2,500 shares valued at $50. The directors purchased 120 shares.

In February 1865, The Kingston and Rondout Railroad Company became a corporate entity under the General Act of 1850. Stockholders appointed the following officers of the new company: Thomas Cornell, president; Henry D. H. Snyder, vice president; and William C. More, secretary and treasurer. In October it purchased the Union Plank Road Company for $25,000, which gave the horse railroad the franchise and right-of-way for its line. Company stock was advertised as available from the First National Bank of Rondout.

The same month, the Rondout Board of Village Trustees granted permission for the railroad company to build a single track with the necessary passing sidings from Garden to Ferry Streets, through Ferry to Division Street (present-day Broadway) and along Division and Union Avenue to the village boundary. The tracks were to be located in the middle of the streets. The trustees also stipulated that the track could not hinder the passage of wagons and other vehicles. The terminus in Rondout was the Powell dock. By mid-November, subscribers in Rondout purchased $30,000 of the $31,250 worth of stock sold, demonstrating their faith in the new mode of travel and reflecting the ascendancy of their community during this period.

A survey made for the company showed that there was a rise of 188 feet over a distance of 4,050 feet from the corner of Ferry and Division Streets to Chestnut Street. This did not include rocky

O'Reilly's Hill. Beyond Chestnut Street, the route was level between Swalbach's and Brown's hotels.

Work on the road commenced May 30, 1866. Officials of the company hoped their cars would run by July. In early June, the directors announced the purchase of three one-horse cars and two two-horse cars from a railroad in New Jersey and awarded a contract to J. H. Tuthill for 4,000 ties.

Early in July, two horse cars arrived in Rondout on the steamer *James Madison*. By mid-July, workers had finished grading and almost finished placing Tuthill's ties. Some rails were in place and the directors confidently expressed the opinion that the railroad would begin operating around the first of August, though their rail supplier was tardy in his delivery. The company also announced that all of the cars had arrived and were being repaired and repainted.

Toward the end of July, people at the west end of Kingston started to grumble. The terminus in Kingston was at North Front and Green Streets. At the time of the stock sale, the directors promised people on the west end that the line would extend to their area. The west-end residents threatened to boycott the line because this promise was not kept.

By the middle of July the rails had arrived, but one trouble spot—a stubborn ledge near O'Reilly's Hill—required much blasting and delayed the start of operations until September 16. At this time, the horse railroad purchased the omnibus line from Jacob Rider who was then appointed superintendent of the new operation. The directors were on hand for the maiden trip over the new rail bed to insure all was in good running order. With Jona Keiffer as operator, the first horse car ran from Rondout to the Kingston terminus in thirty-five minutes, excluding stops. The trip covered three miles. The return trip from Green to the Powell dock took twenty-five minutes. The proud directors declared the line to be in perfect order. That afternoon, the horse railroad was opened to the public and carried 518 passengers. More than thirteen hundred passengers used the railroad during the following two days. It was a fine start, but within two weeks passengers complained that the cars were not running on schedule.

Uptown—Downtown; Horsecars—Trolley Cars

The fare was ten cents from Rondout to Kingston or from Kingston to Rondout. Travel within Kingston or Rondout cost five cents. P. M. Gaasbeck sold commuter tickets at eleven tickets for a dollar. Student tickets allowed twenty rides for a dollar. Cars ran every half hour from 5:00 A.M. to midnight. In November, a non-transferable commutation ticket was introduced allowing the purchaser up to fifty rides within a calendar month for $2.50. That month the company extended the line to the corner of Bridge and Taylor Streets in West Kingston.

During April 1867, the company had two platform cars built. These cars, costing $1,000 each, were placed in service in early May 1867. The gross earnings for that month were $1,900. During July, the horse railroad expended considerable energy to maintain and improve its tracks. It paved all the principal crossings with cobble stones and filled other places with hard material. The first reported accident involving horse cars took place in late September 1867 during a special event in Kingston. Two cars collided without damage or injuries.

In January the following year, stockholders elected a new board, with Thomas Cornell again president. Samuel D. Coykendall became secretary, and by autumn, a two percent dividend was declared. In July 1868, the company encountered problems still found in public transportation today. A letter from a patron complained of the profane language and foul body and breath odors encountered in the cars. The profanity, the writer reported, caused lady passengers to flee. Another complaint was against a man who persisted playing a kettle drum. The complainer suggested that the company do something or risk losing patronage. To the discomfort of the temperate, inebriated passengers often boarded the cars. It also was reported that the conductors on cars 8 and 9 liked to sing; apparently their off-key renditions were not a hit with their passengers, who suggested the singing conductors practice more in private. Complaints in later years concerned the arrogance of drivers who would ignore requests to board or sometimes would not halt at a designated stop.

Horse droppings at stopping points caused undesirable odors, and the recommendation was that the company should keep chloride of lime sprinkled on these spots, but this, too, had its drawbacks: So much lime was spread by 1880 that passengers reported a horse car lost in a lime-dust storm near city hall. The driver said he did not dare drink water for a week for fear he would "slake and crumble" due to the lime dust he inhaled on Union Avenue.

The Kingston and Rondout Horse Railroad Company announced a fare increase on August 15, 1868 because of the increased cost of feed and replacement horses):

Through fare (from Rondout to Kingston) . . . . 12 cents
Way fare (within either village) . . . . 7 cents
Student fare (within either village) . . . . 7 cents
Ten-ride ticket $1

By any measure, the horse railroad was successful: During October, receipts for each day were never less than $60 and might run as high as $250. The following year, during which the company paved its track through Fair Street, saw monthly incomes of $1,161 to $1,530. In February 1870, a new fare structure was again announced:

Through fare. . . . . 12 cents or ten tickets for $1
Way fare . . . . 6 cents or 20 tickets for $1
Monthly commutation tickets . . . . 50 trips for $4

A new, red ten-cent passenger ticket was found to be counterfeited, and new tickets were printed immediately to replace the red fakes. In June, new tokens made of rubber and about the size of the then-current two-cent piece were issued. Way tokens were black; through tokens were red.

More important than counterfeit tickets, horse droppings, unruly passengers and singing or arrogant conductors, the principal impediments to a smooth operation were the problems of guiding horse cars down slippery, sloping rails and removing snow in the winter. Division Street was especially tricky for drivers on wet days when horses were apt to lose their footing going down the slope. One wag suggested using balky horses that did not want to go anyway and would surely take their time going down hill. Winter was especially hard for horse cars. During the worst weather, sleighs replaced the cars. In 1869, Henry W. Winne, an omnibus operator, ran sleighs in competition with the horse railroad company. The sleighing season in Kingston averaged seven weeks.

Snow shoveling caused friction between the company and its neighbors along the right-of-way. Shovelers sometimes piled the snow from the tracks in front of homes. In retaliation, some homeowners would shovel the snow back on the tracks. Children packed down the snow with their sleds and toboggans, making track clearing more difficult. Sometimes battle lines were drawn between merchants along Division Street (lower Broadway) and horse car railroad shovelers. The merchants usually lost because they were outnumbered and outshoveled.

Superintendent Jacob Rider was proud that his tracks stayed open during heavy snows, like those in January 1873, though it meant treacherous going for sleighs wherever his crews piled snow. In early February 1873, owners of the Music Hall in Kingston arranged for ample horse car transportation to bring attendees to a special performance and return them to Rondout. A week later the weather warmed up and melting snow required laborers to bail water off the tracks with scoop shovels. The next week another heavy snow hit and the *Freeman* estimated that it cost the horse railroad $2,000 to keep its tracks open.

In April 1870, the horse railroad granted permission to the Rondout & Oswego Railroad (later the Ulster & Delaware) to use its track to the Cornell storehouse. (Thomas Cornell was also president of the Rondout & Oswego.) The steam line agreed to put down a T-rail. In November, another two-percent dividend was declared. While ridership declined in the winter months, the summer trade was lively enough to allow the dividend. During the following year, platform cars began to replace earlier models known as "humpbacks," and a new color scheme featuring shades of green replaced the original "dingy yellow."

Henry W. Winne continued to run his omnibus operation but apparently coveted the horse railroad, for in February 1872 he offered to lease the railroad at six percent for ten years. This was a better offer than made by a rival, the Sutterlee Group, but it apparently came to naught, as did a renewed offer in September for a lease at seven percent. When rejected by the directors, Winne threatened to take his offer directly to the stockholders.

Meanwhile, passenger complaints about service and conductors continued. One passenger wrote to the newspaper that it took an hour and twenty-five minutes to get from Rondout to Kingston. In April, the company announced it would run its cars on a twenty-minute schedule, and patronage increased. (Before the improved service, passengers frequently could walk to their destinations faster than waiting for the next horse car.) Apparently the demeanor of the conductors remained the same, however, for complaints escalated the next year. In July, a doctor trying to board a car he expected to stop lost his balance and fell in the mud.

The company continued to prosper and to improve its tracks and its rolling stock. It declared a dividend of three percent in September 1873, and in October, reduced the pay of drivers by twenty-five cents a day. The same month, the company purchased land known as the Russell property on the corner of Washington Avenue and North Front Street. It planned to use this property for a depot. It continued to run horse cars to the depot of the New York, Kingston & Syracuse Railroad (successor to the Rondout & Oswego and the future Ulster & Delaware) to connect with passenger trains.

Horse car drivers proved to be resourceful individuals. On December 30, 1873, the locomotive John C. Broadhead of the New York, Kingston & Syracuse had a slight accident and blocked the horse-car tracks. The driver jumped the rails and proceeded up Garden Street (where there were no tracks) to Division Street. Here he drove the horses back on the rails. About two weeks later, a wagon loaded with thirty-foot planks lost its load which ended up across the track. Again the driver jumped the track, went around the obstruction, and continued on his way after regaining the rails.

Several new, smaller cars were introduced in 1874. They featured patented collection boxes that eliminated the need for conductors and could be pulled by one horse (except on Division Street). In addition, four new platform cars were built.

Uptown—Downtown; Horsecars—Trolley Cars

The horse railroad company served an important link in Kingston's transportation system. Going from Rondout to Kingston, the horse cars connected with steam trains. Going to Rondout they connected with steamboats such as the *Baldwin* and *Cornell* and the ferry to Rhinecliff which, in turn, connected with trains to New York and Albany. The horse railroad scheduled its service to accommodate these connections. To aid workers from Kingston bound for Rondout, Superintendent Dumont added a 5:20 A.M. departure in April 1874. To alleviate the fears of his passengers, Dumont used heavy timbers to repair a retaining wall on Union Avenue just above New Kirk Avenue, where the track ran above and close to a sidewalk.

Several events took place in June 1874. The horse railroad put in an iron turntable near the Rhinecliff ferry dock, and in upper Kingston it built a loop in the stable. This eliminated the need for hitching and unhitching horses at the end of the line. Three of six new cars built by John Stephanson in New York were shipped to Rondout via the steamer *Marshall*, and the others arrived in short order on the steamer *A. B. Valentine*. Painted a light yellow, the new cars boasted J. B. S. Sanson's patented fare boxes. They were put into service within a week.

The elimination of conductors was not a blessing as far as passengers were concerned. The driver was too busy attending to his horses and watching for passengers arriving and departing to control the drunks in his car. Ladies arriving from New York on the night boat were subjected to insults and obscene language by these louts. This lead to the suggestion that the company put an extra employee, preferably a strong one, on the horse cars at night. Passengers also complained about the smaller capacity of the new cars and requested that the company add more cars or run more frequently.

On August 11, 1874, Henry W. Winne finally got his stake in the railroad. He purchased 1,350 shares of stock in the Kingston and Rondout Horse Railroad Company at $25 per share from Thomas Cornell. This gave Winne controlling interest. Because the Winne family was a large one, it was rumored that they would all now ride for free. At its reorganization meeting of August 13 the following directors resigned: Thomas Cornell, James G. Lindsley, Anthony

Benson, Hiram Schoonmaker, Michael J. Madden, Charles Bray, John Hussey and Samuel D. Coykendall. The following were elected to fill their places: Henry W. Winne, Davis Winne, William Winne, Samuel P. Dimmick, Cornelius C. Winne, Benjamin J. Winne, Rueben Bernard and Manasseh Longyear. The old directors remaining on the board were William Lounsberry, Elias T. Van Nostrand, Artemas Sahler and Patrick J. Flynn. In addition, the new directors elected the following officials: Reuben Bernard, president; Chauncey Keator, secretary; C. H. Van Gaasbeck, treasurer. The executive committee consisted of Samuel P. Dimmick, Benjamin J. Winne and Cornelius C. Winne. The committee appointed Henry W. Winne, superintendent.

 Two rumors circulated at the time the Winne-heavy management began to set policy: that horse cars would run on Sunday and that the cars would cease running to Higginsville (the area from the hollow behind Front Street to Esopus Creek). The first proved to be true. Horse cars ran on Sunday for the first time since the start of the line. They ran every hour starting at 7:00 A.M. and continuing to 9:00 P.M. Because of the wide acceptance of the Sunday cars, Winne planned to increase the number of trips. Many Kingston people rode horse cars to Rondout to attend Sunday evening services. The new management also announced a new fare structure, but it is difficult to see its difference from the previous system. At the time it apparently engendered some unhappiness among passengers. New tickets cost five cents and were good in either village; two tickets were required to go between the villages.

 In the middle of a day in October, a Wallkill Valley Railroad train smashed into a horse car. No injuries were reported. In another incident a horse car was ready to leave on its 3:00 P.M. trip from Rondout. The noise from a nearby New York, Kingston & Syracuse engine startled the horses, and they took off. Luckily the driver, Hiram Barnhart, caught up with the runaways and stopped them.

 The new superintendent had his hands full repairing and upgrading tracks. His men filled holes and leveled the space between the rails. Observers reported that the workers put the track in excellent condition. Reacting to a complaint about boys hanging on the rear platforms of cars, Winne hired an officer to arrest anyone caught hitching free rides. He announced that during the winter he would introduce a heated car, and in January 1875 the first heated car made its appearance, to the delight of its passengers.

Another improvement was the addition of a third horse on cars to ease the ascent up Division Street. Even this was not enough during severe icing conditions, like those of mid-February 1875. As a safety precaution during such times, the horse car company employed sleighs to bring its patrons up Division Street. The woes that winter multiplied. Much salt was used, often to little effect. In March, a horse car jumped the track on Wall Street and crashed into a lamp post in front of the State of New York National Bank. A few days later snow caused problems. Superintendent Winne himself ran a snowplow with a six-horse team. Reportedly it just kept snowing, and he kept plowing. The shoveling contest continued between the railroad's snow shovelers and the homeowners along the track. But by the end of March, warming conditions brought a return to normal.

To accommodate commuters, Winne added an extra car in May 1875 that left Kingston at 6:20 A.M. and Rondout at 7:20 A.M. He also tried to abolish the way fare (the rate charged to travel within one of the communities), but his customers apparently let him know that they would rather walk than spend ten cents for a short ride. He returned to the way-fare system four days after his revenues decreased. He agreed with the owners of the steamers *James W. Baldwin* and *Thomas Cornell* to meet their boats from New York; in August he had a new, extra-large platform built to accommodate passengers arriving by steamboats and trains. An open car with room for fifty passengers was put in service, and because of its success the company built three more. Awnings were added as a refinement.

Drivers were bedeviled by youngsters who would hitch rides on the backs of the cars, sometimes annoying passengers with profanity. At other times they would run alongside, shouting that someone was hitching a ride, and would keep this up until the driver stopped the car and walked to the rear, only to discover no one was there. When two cars passed each other, drivers checked the passing car for freeloaders; some of these felt the whip of the passing driver.

Because of his trouble the previous winter, Superintendent Winne decided to install runners under his humpback cars. In their first test they proved so successful that regular horse cars were no longer used until the snow melted. The runner-mounted humpbacks ran on time and were comfortable, and the company avoided the considerable expense of clearing the streets. Another profitable move was the acquisition from Manasseh Longyear of the contract to carry mail between Kingston and Rondout. On the down side, one or two of the local lager beer saloons used tokens in their establishments that were very similar to the horse railroad tokens. When a passenger deposited his fare, it was difficult for the driver to see whether it was a lager token or a horse railroad token. The company accumulated enough lager tokens to keep all of the drivers in beer for a couple of days.

In 1876, Winne had an additional siding installed on Fair Street near the Surrogate's office and one on Ferry Street so cars would not have to wait on the road. He continued to tinker with the way fare and finally agreed to accept five cents in cash in lieu of a ticket. Another Winne improvement was the installation of a siding at the Wallkill Valley Railroad station. A car could wait there for train arrivals without blocking the main track. Working two cars at a time, he began a program of repainting and repairs. He continued to use the big platform cars instead of the regular horse cars.

Was his management sound? Were his efforts at preventive maintenance enough? The complaint most often heard was that the horse cars did not run on schedule, and events proved that storm clouds were gathering for the superintendent. James Van Buren offered to buy the company from Winne in August 1876, and Winne accepted the offer, but Van Buren backed out at signing time.

In November, the directors announced a new schedule, with horse cars running on Sundays only to meet boats at Rondout. They planned to run covered sleighs on stormy days, and four days later the first snow arrived along with the sleighs. Ice and snow continued to plague the line that winter. The first horse car of 1877 ran on February 3. When workers attempted to remove ice for the horse car wheels, sleighs got stuck in the ruts.

In a fatal move, the directors voted on March 21 to issue $15,000 worth of first-mortgage bonds of $500 each, payable in ten years. These bonds were to pay seven percent semiannually. The purpose of the issue, according to the directors, was to pay off a floating indebtedness of approximately $9,000. Reaction was swift. Sarah More, William Lounsberry, Charles D. Bruyn, Peter Masten, James O. Merritt, George B. Merritt, Andrew Near, Cornelius Burhans, Catherine Ludlum, Augustus Bruyn and Luke Noone joined together as plaintiffs and secured an injunction on April 3 to restrain the company from mortgaging the road. The plaintiffs asked that a receiver be appointed because they believed the real reason for the bonding was to wipe out company stock and sell the road "for the benefit of specific persons" and that the financial condition of the road did not show bonding was necessary. Winne reputedly said that the plaintiffs did not care about the road but just wanted him out. On April 11, Judge Osborne in Albany found that there were not sufficient grounds shown for the appointment of a receiver and revoked the injunction, ruling that the board of directors had a legal right to issue bonds.

In August, a fire broke out in the sash-and-blind factory of Charles Miner. It destroyed Miner's building along with two others, including the stables of the horse railroad. The company arranged to use the sheds of Wilbur Hale on Chester Street near Union Avenue. The following year, with permission of the common council, it leased a barn belonging to Horace Humphrey after receiving an insurance settlement of $1,475.

The ever-evolving enterprise made several changes in 1878 and 1879, after the usual winter troubles abated. Cars were scheduled to run every ten minutes, but the line to Higginsville was terminated due to low patronage. Only one car ran on Sunday to meet the steamer *James W. Baldin* at 5:00 P.M. Smoking was banned on all cars (drivers had to enforce the ban or risk discharge). The company drove posts, about ten inches long, inside the rails in an effort to keep people off the horse car track. These posts presented an obstruction that could damage a vehicle.

Late in September 1877, S. S. Westbrook auctioned $4,000 worth of company stock. Davis Winne, the only bidder, picked it up for $1,000, possibly indicating the extent of public confidence in the road at this time. New legal challenges to Winne and the railroad arose. In April 1878, Artemas Sahler, William M. Hayes and other stockholders sued. This time the plaintiffs wanted the election of all the directors (except E. T. Van Nostrand and Patrick J. Flynn) declared without authority, a new election ordered, a receiver appointed, and Henry W. Winne restrained from voting on certain shares of stock. Further, the plaintiffs claimed that the defendants had allowed the condition of the road to deteriorate and unnecessary indebtedness to be incurred. The defendants denied all claims, and the case was thrown out of court.

An example of dereliction on the company's part was the condition of the track on Union Avenue. It was out of gauge because the sleepers (ties) had decayed badly. Heat from the summer sun caused the rails to warp because of the lack of support. At a special meeting in August, the directors reduced Winne's powers by taking away his right to sell, trade or otherwise dispose of horses except by an order of the executive committee.

The following year, the company was found to be in default on its first mortgage bonds. The court ordered Referee William T. Holt to sell the horse railroad. Holt scheduled the sale for late April 1879, but he postponed the sale three times because there were no bidders. On May 13, 1879, the sale finally took place at the Court House. To nobody's surprise, the bidders were Thomas Cornell and Henry W. Winne. The bidding progressed to $10,100 (a bid by Winne that he immediately withdrew). Thomas Cornell then bought the horse railroad company for $10,100. The judgment against the company had been $17,000 (the $15,000 mortgage plus accrued interest).

The transfer to Cornell took place on May 16. The directors temporarily appointed William H. DeGarmo, a former county treasurer, as superintendent. A *Freeman* editorial suggested the new owner rebuild the tracks and obtain new cars. New rails were on order by the end of the month, a new schedule that met the approval of the public was in place, and new fare rates were established:

Uptown—Downtown; Horsecars—Trolley Cars

12 through tickets	$1
10 school tickets	fifty cents
11 way tickets	fifty cents

For the public, the important thing was keeping on schedule. Under the Winne regime, passengers had to leave for a horse car stop up to fifteen minutes before the scheduled time to avoid missing the car. The new schedule called for a twenty-minute interval between cars and additional cars to wait for the arrival of steamers at night.

By mid-August workers had laid new rails from St. James Street down Union Avenue to the top of Rondout hill. The new company installed two short sidings (called switches) on each side of the railroad crossing, instead of the long switch previously in place on Union Avenue. On September 22, all cars stopped running while workers made the connections with the new track. The company sent stages to meet the steamers *Mary Powell* and *James W. Baldwin*. Work continued through the evening by the light of bonfires. Later, workers installed a switch at the corner of St. James and Fair Streets, replacing the one opposite the surrogate's office. A crew of 150 put the track on Ferry Street in place. By the end of November, work was completed. The horse railroad continued to cater to Music Hall patrons. In December, cars were available to carry attendees of the comic opera *The Doctor of Alcantara* to and from Rondout.

As the year 1880 unfolded, the new management, in a public relations move, ordered blue caps for its drivers and managed to keep the line on schedule despite snow and cold. Because heated car Number 4 was so popular with patrons, the company supplied several other cars with heaters. Drivers liked them, especially when they had to wait at the turntable on a cold night. Another popular innovation was the posting of timetables in each car for the Rhinecliff ferry *Lark*, and the extension of awnings on the open cars to protect the drivers (which also helped to keep rain from blowing on passengers). By July, the company was running on a ten-minute schedule week days between 10:00 A.M. and 8:00 P.M., but complaints about arrogant drivers continued.

There is no twentieth-century equivalent for some medical practices of this period. Dr. Hyman Rosa extracted a tooth from Bub Terwilliger while they were aboard one of the cars. A short time later, Dr. Rosa boarded Chris Shader's car. Shader was obviously in much pain. Dr. Rosa reached into his black bag, found his forceps and removed the tooth that was causing the trouble right on the spot, horrifying the car's only passenger. One of the drivers' problems still resonates: how to enforce the ban against smoking. More than once, burly drivers used physical intimidation to curtail cigar smoking on their cars.

To promote the horse railroad, half-fare rates were available to any person who had a round-trip ticket on the *Mary Powell*. This meant a Kinston or Rondout resident could go from home all the way to New York City and back for $1.10. It was only a three-minute walk from the end of the track to the *Mary Powell*'s new dock.

Lighted cars ("enough light to read by"), built in Schenectady, were introduced in September 1880. Other cars, manufactured in Rochester, were added in April 1881. By then, the company owned forty-two horses and employed thirteen men in the stable. The horses traveled an average of twenty miles per day and were sometimes kept busy until 2:00 A.M. when there were performances or charity parties at the Samson Opera House in Rondout. (See Appendix B for time table.) That year the directors declared a dividend of four percent.

In 1882, maintenance crews painted the cars' running gear a brilliant red and replaced aging rubber springs with steel springs. New cars were added, and unused rails removed from Green Street. Horse cars provided transportation to the armory for devotees of a new fad, roller skating. Large crowds would skate while a band played lively music.

In early July, a driver had one John McNalty arrested for vagrancy and using bad language in the presence of ladies on his car. McNalty was found guilty and sent to the penitentiary in Albany for three months because he couldn't pay his $15 fine.

Overleaf: Horsecar in the midst of a Barnum and Bailey circus parade on Broadway, 1885. Courtesy Joseph Fautz.

Uptown—Downtown; Horsecars—Trolley Cars

Urban Transportation in Kingston, New York, 1866-1930

UPTOWN—DOWNTOWN; HORSECARS—TROLLEY CARS

By May 1884, the horse railroad opened a new waiting room at the junction on Union Avenue for passengers arriving on West Shore trains. From there cars ran to both Rondout and Kingston. Horse cars stopped so often at Decatur's corner to allow passengers to disembark for the Eagle Hotel it was said that the horses would automatically slow, whether there was a passenger for that stop or not.

To the end of its days, the horse railroad seems to have done its best to accommodate passengers bound for performances, circuses, ball games and special events such as steamer excursions to Coney Island. During the school year, youngsters rode the affectionately dubbed "scholar's car" each morning at 8:40. Connections with the Hudson River steamer *Mary Powell* were convenient—the horse railroad line terminated a three-minute walk from the *Mary Powell*'s new dock.

In a notable change from earlier years, passengers commented that the drivers were polite, attentive, neat and clean looking though smoking on the cars remained an issue. Improvements in its mature years included the addition of a "salt car" for winter use, extension of the line up Fair to North Front and onto Wall Street (North Front Street then became the center of business activity uptown and rails were removed from John Street), a turntable on Wall Street (which allowed passengers to disembark while the car was on the turntable) and replacement of worn rails with steel rails over the entire length of the line. Cushions and center lamps were added, and new cars (described by the company as "handsome") were purchased. The police department abandoned its much criticized practice of transporting prisoners on horse cars.

The maintenance of safe crossings was always an issue. The horse-car company had given the West Shore Railroad permission to cross its tracks. In return, the West Shore agreed to put the crossing in first-class condition, but this was not done until late 1891. In July 1885, a near-accident occurred at the West Shore crossing on Broadway. A car bound for Kingston stopped at the crossing because an engine was passing. Apparently the gateman raised the gates prematurely, for when the horse car reached the north track the driver heard three sharp whistles. He immediately applied his whip and succeeded in completing the crossing just as the Saratoga Express, applying its air brakes, passed behind him.

The great snow storm of March 11 to 13, 1888, will always be recalled as the "Blizzard of '88." In Kingston, snow covered the ground to a depth of about three feet, with drifts from twelve to fifteen feet high. By four o'clock on March 11, the horse railroad stopped running. When the snow finally stopped on March 13, four horses were need to pull each car. Even diligent shoveling left places where the snow lifted the wheels of the cars off the tracks.

By November 1891, rumors started to fly about the possible electrification of the line. Samuel D. Coykendall denied that the horse railroad had been sold to New York City interests who intended to install a double-track electric trolley line that would extend as far as Higginsville. The word on the street was that the asking price for the railroad was $175,000, however, by March the following year, Coykendall himself was ready to transform his line into the new mode of transport.

UPTOWN—DOWNTOWN; HORSECARS—TROLLEY CARS

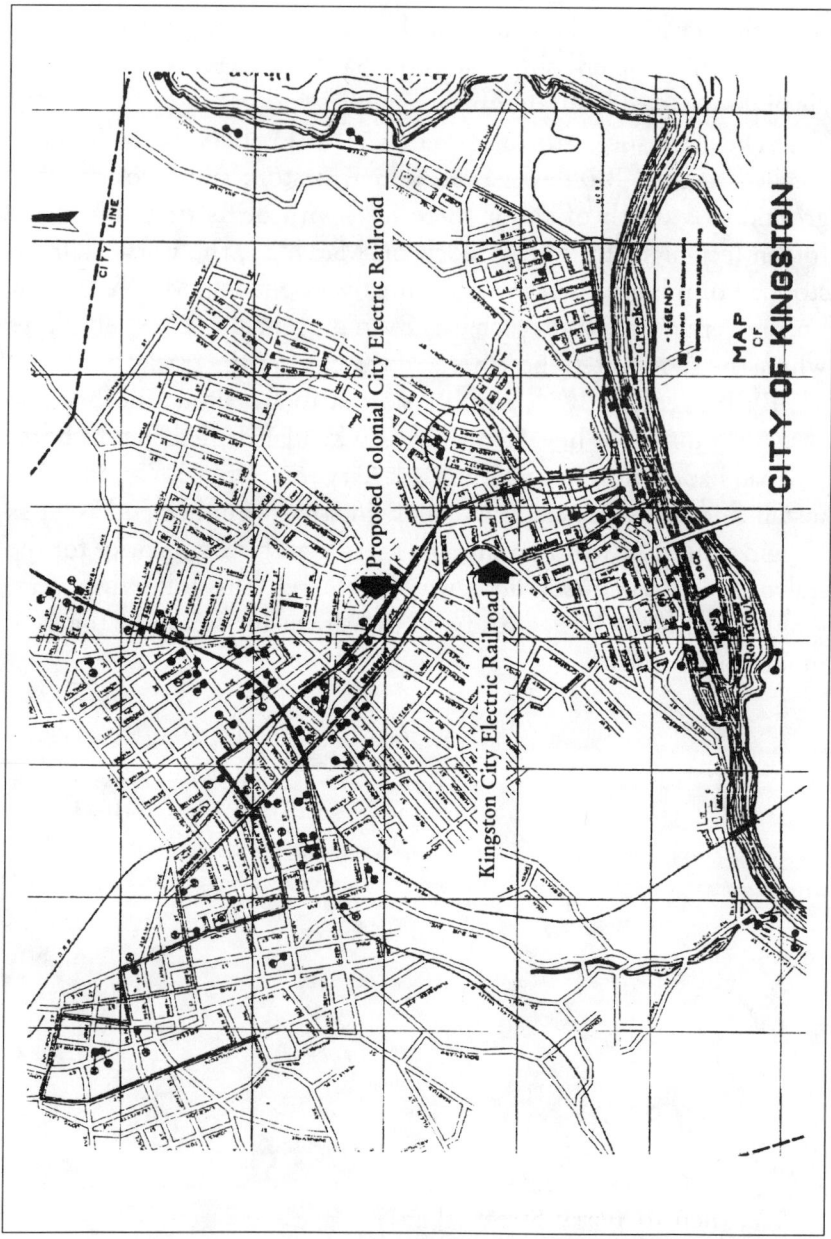

Map of theKingston City Electric Railroad and
the proposed Colonial City Electric Railroad.
Courtesy The Trolley Museum of New York (map modified by the author)

Kingston's Great Trolley Fight: Kingston City Electric Railway vs. Colonial City Railroad

THE ORDINARINESS OF TODAY'S URBAN PUBLIC TRANSPORTAtion makes it difficult to understand the passion with which the media and the traveling public embraced electric trolleys in their first years. Minute details of trolley line construction and operation were eagerly reported by Kingston and Rondout newspapers, and a fifteen-minute delay in service brought reporters scurrying to discover the cause. The big story, however, was the rivalry between two competing lines: the Kingston City Electric Railway Company and the Colonial City Railroad Company.

On March 17, 1892, the Kingston City Electric Railway Company was incorporated in New York State to operate an "electric street-surface railroad" for 2.97 miles from its western terminus on North Front Street to Fair Street, to St. James Street, to Union Avenue, then to Ferry Street, then to an eastern terminus at the junction of Ferry Street and the Strand.

The company issued capital stock of $175,000 divided into 1,750 shares of $100 each. The stockholders elected the following directors for the first year: Edward T. Stelle, E. H. Laughran, C. W. Deyo, W. Scott Gillespie, E. G. Lawrence, A. F. Winne, Robert Wilson and George T. Smith of Kingston, and James Hasbrouck of Rondout. Later that month, Kingston Mayor David Kennedy appointed James G. Tubby, A. H. Crosby and Henry H. Pitts to visit cities where electric trolley systems were in use and to report back to the common council on the prospects.

On June 4, N. C. Powelson of a rival company, the Colonial City Electric Railroad, submitted a petition to the common council requesting consent for the construction, maintenance and operation of an electric railroad. The new company proposed starting on the Strand at Abruyn Street, running to Hasbrouck Avenue, to the West Shore depot, through Tremper Avenue to O'Neill Street, through O'Neill Street, crossing Union Avenue, through Henry Street to Clinton Avenue, up Clinton Avenue to Main Street, through Main Street to Wall Street, through Wall Street to North Front Street, through North Front Street to Washington Avenue, and through Washington Avenue to a terminus at the corner of Linderman Avenue.

The following week, Samuel D. Coykendall informed the common council that his Kingston City Railroad wanted to change from horse power to electric power, to rebuild the horse railroad tracks and to reduce the fare to a uniform rate of five cents for travel to any point within the system. Further, he said that his company had no problem if the common council wanted to grant permission for a trolley line to run on every street and avenue in Kingston if it were good for the city. However, he cautioned against granting permission to any company whose proposed line would cross that of the steam railroad at grade. (The Kingston and Rondout Horse Railroad had tracks in place on Union Avenue [Broadway] before the West Shore Railroad entered Kingston.) At first, Mayor Kennedy held up the franchising of the Colonial City line, but during July the council notified Colonial to file its bond and note by August 3 or a resolution granting the franchise would be invalid. On August 1, the Colonial City Railroad Company filed a $20,000 bond with Kingston City Clerk Schepmoes and identified its bondsman.

By the end of August, workmen began excavating the cellar of a new powerhouse for Colonial. An engine made by Ball and Wood Company, of Elizabeth, New Jersey, and some wire had arrived. The firm of Campbell and Dempsey had the contract to build the powerhouse. It ordered 175,000 bricks from William Hutton and started the brickwork in September. By November, two new boilers were in place and the engine assembled. Finally, interior woodwork was completed and rails ordered from a Johnstown manufacturer.

Meanwhile, the Kingston City Electric Railroad issued an annual report showing a surplus of $15,304.21. (See Appendix C—this represented only the horse railroad operation.)

At 6:30 P.M. on October 6, a milk train backing across Broadway crashed into a Kingston City horse car. Fortunately, the crash did not injure either James Norton, the driver, or Chester Merritt, the only passenger. The milk train struck the rear end of the horse car, knocking in three panels. The accident demonstrated the danger that existed at this intersection. From the time the West Shore Railroad applied for permission to cross the Kingston and Rondout (later Kingston City) Horse Railroad's tracks, people complained that a crossing at grade level was inviting disaster. (An underpass for vehicular traffic there was not completed until 1952.)

As the two companies jockeyed for position in late November 1892, the Colonial City Railway Company petitioned the common council to amend its trolley line franchise. The proposed change would route the line through Hasbrouck Avenue to Grand Street, then through Grand to Smith Avenue, through Smith to Cornell Street, through Cornell across Union Avenue to Cedar Street, and then through Cedar Street. The common council required a new bond because of the changes.

In early February the next year, the directors of the Kingston City Railroad announced that construction of their electric trolley line would begin when the frost was out of the ground. By late March, work on the powerhouse on the Strand was progressing. In April, crews started taking up the old rails and raised the tops of the doorways in the old horse-car barn to accommodate the higher electric cars. New rails were laid, starting at the ferry dock. A temporary turntable was installed in the street in front of the *Freeman* office in Rondout. Work continued a section at a time with a transfer point at the section under construction. The line purchased approximately 1,000 rails and other materials from the Pennsylvania Steel Company of Philadelphia. The new rails were installed flush with the street and "spring frogs" were employed in the design of the switches. A survey showed the line to be 2.77 miles long. To speed rail laying, the work crew was doubled. Many of the workers had laid rail through the difficult Stony Clove Notch in the Catskills above Phoenicia and understood the craft. Some horse-railroad ties 25 years old were found to be still sound, although all were replaced.

An exceptionally high tide left the ground along Ferry Street wet and muddy, slowing work. New rail had been laid as far as the Mansion House by April 18, and the old track and ties removed on Union Avenue above Abeel Street. The depression of 1893 caused many companies to fail. Among the casualties was the Pennsylvania Steel Company. Fortunately, all of the equipment and most of the rails ordered had been delivered. In early May, iron poles for the electric lines arrived, and by May 10 the men removing paving stones, rails and ties had reached the West Shore tracks. They were followed by rail layers and, at a slower pace, pavers and installers of poles and wires.

Meanwhile, the powerhouse was progressing. Two Payne-Corliss engines of 500 horsepower each were designed to drive two multipolar Thompson and Houston type 100 generators, which furnished the electricity necessary to run the cars.

The Kingston City line ordered six new cars from the Pullman Company's plant in Pullman, Illinois. The cars were equipped with waterproof, twenty-five-horsepower General Electric motors based on Thompson and Houston patterns. The cars were twenty-five feet long and were lighted and heated by electricity. They were governed by two controlling switches that could make the car stop in twelve and a half feet. Also, the motor could be reversed, stopping the car

Opposite page: Wagon-mounted, wire-installation platform.
Courtesy The Trolley Museum of New York

almost instantly. Because they were double-enders (the motorman could run the car from either end), they eliminated the need for turntables at the ends of the line.

Copper wire, weighing almost a pound per yard, transmitted electricity to the trolley cars. A dead guard wire protected the copper from electric light wires in case it should break or fall. Installation of the electrical equipment was overseen by W. W. Vaughan of the General Electric Company. Working from a seventeen-foot-high platform mounted on a wagon running on the new tracks, crews suspended Kingston's first trolley wire, and by May 15, 1893, the first trolley ran on the lower section of the line.

The rest of the month saw feverish activity as the track layers followed on the heels of track removers. Workers took up the turntable on North Front Street. For the convenience of its customers, the line operated stages, and where the rails were completed, horse cars. June saw the arrival of a Payne-Corliss engine (from B. W. Payne and Sons of Elmira) weighing twenty-two tons. The powerhouse

Above: Dead guard wire above intersection of Kingston trolley and U&D tracks at Hasbrouck Ave. looking south toward Pierpont St.
Courtesy The Trolley Museum of New York
Opposite page: Property owners between Cornell and Thomas Streets.
Courtesy Eugene Dauner

was ready for the engine, the flywheel of which was twelve feet in diameter, thirty-two inches wide and came in four sections.

Work on the track progressed to the point where a horse car could run the entire length of the line by June 7, and stages were discontinued, but the forcasted July 1 opening day proved optimistic. The second engine arrived on June 30 and four of the electric motors for the cars on July 15. A switchboard weighing fourteen hundred pounds also arrived. This equipment controlled the flow of power. On July 28, electricians tested the powerhouse equipment. Workers had painted the engines and dynamos, as well as the thirty-foot by fifty-foot room white. The two Payne-Corliss engines filled most of the space. Their flywheels turned around 150 times per minute. The switchboards contained automatic circuit breakers to stop the flow of electricity in case of a wire break. Lightning arrestors on the switchboard protected equipment in the powerhouse. The boiler

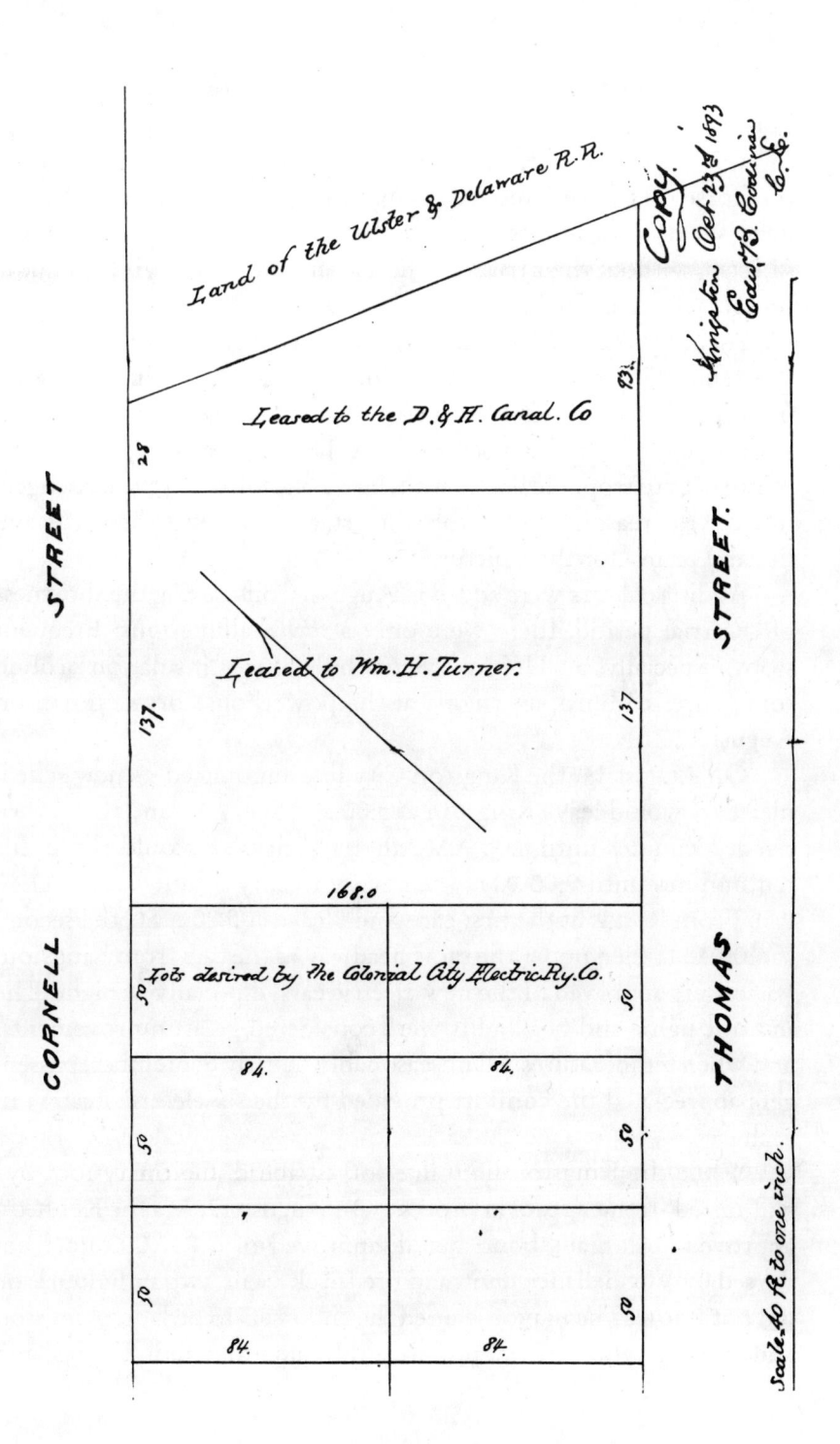

URBAN TRANSPORTATION IN KINGSTON, NEW YORK, 1866-1930

room was twenty-eight by forty-two feet and contained three large boilers.

On August 1, 1893, an electric car began running on the road and the horse cars were removed permanently. All but one of the company's forty-four horses were sold before the end of the month; the old cars, without their trucks (wheel assemblies), were given away to find new lives as chicken coops and play houses.

A card posted in each car informed passengers that the fare was five cents. The cars could run the entire length of the line in twenty minutes. To commemorate the occasion, George Vallette had his photographic equipment set up on St. James Street and signaled the motorman to stop. He had to wait, however, for when the passengers realized the reason for the stop, they started to adjust their hats and ties and primp for their pictures.

Additional cars were added in August. Considering the shortness of the trial period, there were only a few malfunctions: Frequent stops, especially on Union Avenue hill, caused insulation around some wires to burn; an engine at the powerhouse broke down on August 12.

On August 14, the Kingston City line announced its new schedule: Cars would leave Kingston at 5:00 and 5:40 A.M. and then every twenty minutes until 8:00 A.M., after which they would run every ten minutes until 9:00 P.M., then every twenty minutes until 11:40 P.M. From Rondout the first car would leave at 5:20 A.M., the second at 6:00 A.M., then under the same headway as the cars from Kingston. Passengers approved of the new electric cars, especially at night. The interior lights and headlights were considered great improvements, and when temperatures fell unseasonably in early September, passengers appreciated the comfort provided by the six electric heaters in each car.

While the Kingston City line forged ahead, Colonial City was still mired in the approval process. On August 17, Mayor Kennedy approved Colonial's bond but disapproved of a $10,000 note endorsed by Wendell Goodwin and Frederick Swift, two individuals he did not know. The mayor wanted the endorsers to be from Kingston and with known financial resources. His aldermen didn't agree, and the mayor approved the Goodwin-Swift note only after the common council passed a resolution absolving him of any responsibility.

The most famous non-resident involved with Colonial City was Horatio Alger, the author of numerous adventure stories on poor-boy-makes-good themes. His inquiry of late September asking the status of the line attracted the interest of local reporters; Goodwin and Swift replied that they would start construction within ten days and have the line completed by mid-December. The Mercantile Trust Company of New York was said to have arranged a first-mortgage loan of $150,000. Goodwin and Swift agreed to take $100,000 worth of first-mortgage bonds. Local interests were expected to acquire the balance of $50,000.

When a reporter questioned Alger about the number of bonds sold, he answered that subscribers had bought bonds but declined to name them. A *Freeman* reporter learned that no bonds had been sold as of October 4—Colonial City had, in effect, no financial backing. At the same time the *Leader*, perhaps relying on company sources, reported that the sale of bonds was progressing satisfactorily. There was a depression on in 1893, and the sale of bonds, especially for unbuilt electric roads, was difficult.

On October 16, nearly a hundred men, responding to a news article showed up in Ponckhockie looking for construction work on the Colonial City line. No representatives of the company were present, and the men dispersed. This same scene had played several times before with the same result—no jobs.

During the same period, Kingston City had crews at work improving its track, particularly on curved portions, which were banked and brought to uniform radii. The result was a smoother ride. But breakdowns sometimes hindered Kingston City operations. Near the end of October, a power failure caused some passengers to miss their evening trains. On October 26, at the corner of St. James and Broadway, a wooden plug on top of a trolley pole broke. This caused wires and brace wires to fall, delaying service.

In spite of its financial troubles, Colonial City contracted with Reed and McKibben to construct its line. The contractors appointed Alfred Huddler as superintendent and, on November 2, advertised for laborers. This time, between 300 and 400 men gathered at the corner of Washington and Linderman Avenues. N. C. Powelson and Huddler (who was in charge of hiring) greeted the men. Huddler climbed onto a wagon, took out his book and announced he would take down some names. There was such a rush toward the wagon that it almost upset. Huddler managed to take down about fifty names and told the men to report at one o'clock, when tools would arrive. During that morning, teams brought rails to Washington Avenue.

City Engineer Codwise informed Colonial City that its tracks must run down the middle of Washington Avenue to insure that property owners along the avenue could get to the curb in front of their homes, an order that would later cause controversy. He marked the center of the street, and Huddler put a gang of 30 men to work excavating a trench fourteen inches deep to accept the ties and rails. Another twenty men were employed unloading rails. Laborers were paid $1.25 a day.

The sale of Colonial's mortgage bonds was still lagging. As an inducement the line offered to give fifty percent of the bond's face value in common stock. By November 9, the track gang was at work on Cedar Street, and Colonial City found itself ensnared by rock, weather, city politicians and bureaucrats. First, there was considerable disruption to traffic as streets were often impassable. This displeased the aldermen and the city engineer. Then workers encountered rock while excavating the trench on Washington Avenue. The arrival of a sudden snow storm added to Colonial's woes. Citizens complained that trolley tracks crossed sanitary sewer lines, and they worried about who would bear the costs of replacing tracks if the sewers had to be repaired. (This appeared to be the city's problem, because the city engineer had directed Colonial to lay its track in the middle of the thoroughfare across the sewer lines.)

The Kingston City line received a new generator in mid-November. Made by General Electric, it was larger and more powerful than the original equipment, which was not strong enough to stand the strain of running cars up the Broadway hill. The superintendent ordered another new generator.

On November 21, officials of the Colonial line laid off fifty laborers without explanation. One worker, Isaac Van Leuven, swore out a warrant for the arrest of his boss, John Mansfield, on the charge of assault with a shovel and mistreatment of himself and other men. Other labor problems concerned pay: Was a fifty-cent wage reduction (almost half a day's pay) due to shorter daylight hours or to make up for the alleged theft of eighty-six shovels and forty-six picks? Tempers flared, and workers sought relief in court. As a result, the fifty-cent reduction was restored.

Work on the Colonial City line continued during mid-December. Workers installed poles and wires on the Strand near Newark Lime & Cement Company. By that time, they had laid track over the entire line except for a few blocks, but management decided not to extend the line along the Strand to Ponckhockie until spring.

During December 1893, Colonial City employees accidentally damaged the tunnel of the Ulster & Delaware Railroad at the junction of Hasbrouck and Delaware Avenues. The company posted a surety bond of $5,000 to guarantee proper repairs. The following year on April 27, Reed and McKibben sent a letter to H. C. Soop of the Ulster & Delaware, saying that Colonial City had completed the repairs. (See Appendix D.) A huge problem for the company was how to cross the steam railroad tracks. Samuel Coykendall had foretold this problem.

In early January 1894, N. C. Powelson told the press that his line had permission from state railroad commissioners to cross the tracks of the West Shore at grade level, and that he planned to apply to Judge Parker to establish a special commission to decide in what manner the tracks would cross. In truth, the approval granted to Colonial City was only to build the line. Additional state approvals by a special commission would be necessary for the crossing. Meanwhile, electricians ran two engines in Colonial City's powerhouse. They tested satisfactorily. One engine came from Ball Engine Company; the other had been exhibited at the World's Fair.

On January 20, Alva S. Newcomb, representing Colonial City, appeared before Judge D. Cady Herrick of Albany. Newcomb applied to the court for establishment of a special commission to decide

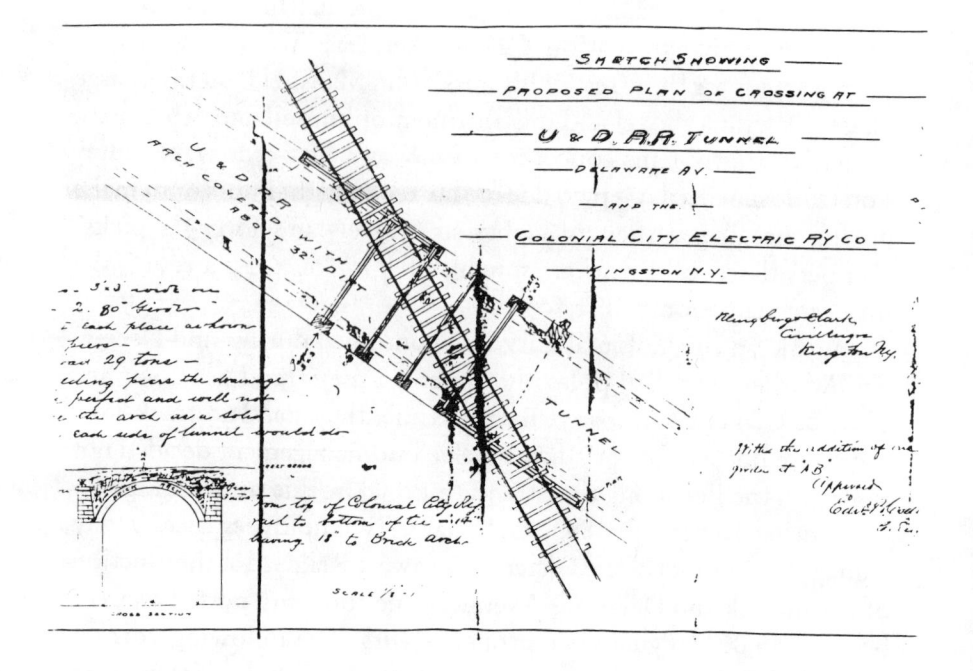

Courtesy Eugene Dauner

where his client would cross the West Shore Railroad tracks and how much the line would have to compensate the railroad. F. L. Westbrook and John J. Linson represented the West Shore Railroad. They argued that under a statute passed the previous winter, Colonial City had to obtain permission from the State Railroad Commission, but the court could appoint a special commission. The judge signed an order to form the commission but cautioned that his order did not mean Colonial City had permission to cross the West Shore's tracks. He then directed Newcomb and the railroad's attorneys to leave the courtroom and decide between themselves on the makeup of the special commission. After much debate, the two parties agreed on Robert A. Snyder of Saugerties, a layman, and former Senator Clarence E. Bloodgood of Catskill, a lawyer. The two sides were unable to agree on an engineer for the commission, so Judge Herrick appointed John J. O'Hara, assistant city engineer of Albany, as the

Colonial City Car #12, an open car.
Courtesy The Trolley Museum of New York

third member. Emory A. Chase, another Catskill lawyer, was appointed to replace Senator Bloodgood, who was ill.

On February 18, Colonial City received six vestibuled cars via the West Shore Railroad. They were manufactured in Missouri by the St. Louis Car Company. Colonial City had the cars painted a very light color, almost white. The cars were enclosed in glass and featured double doors.

In March, both trolley lines announced their intention of running open cars during the summer. Kingston City ordered several such cars from the Pullman Company; Colonial City already had taken delivery of six of seven open cars it had ordered. The company fitted the new cars with Peckham trucks and improved Winkler motors and expected to run them as soon as the frost was out of the ground, assuming permission to cross the West Shore's tracks could be obtained. Colonial City was poised to hire 150 men to connect its two sections.

The special commission's hearing was held on March 23 and 24. Walter M. Houg, chief train dispatcher for the Hudson River Divi-

UPTOWN—DOWNTOWN; HORSECARS—TROLLEY CARS

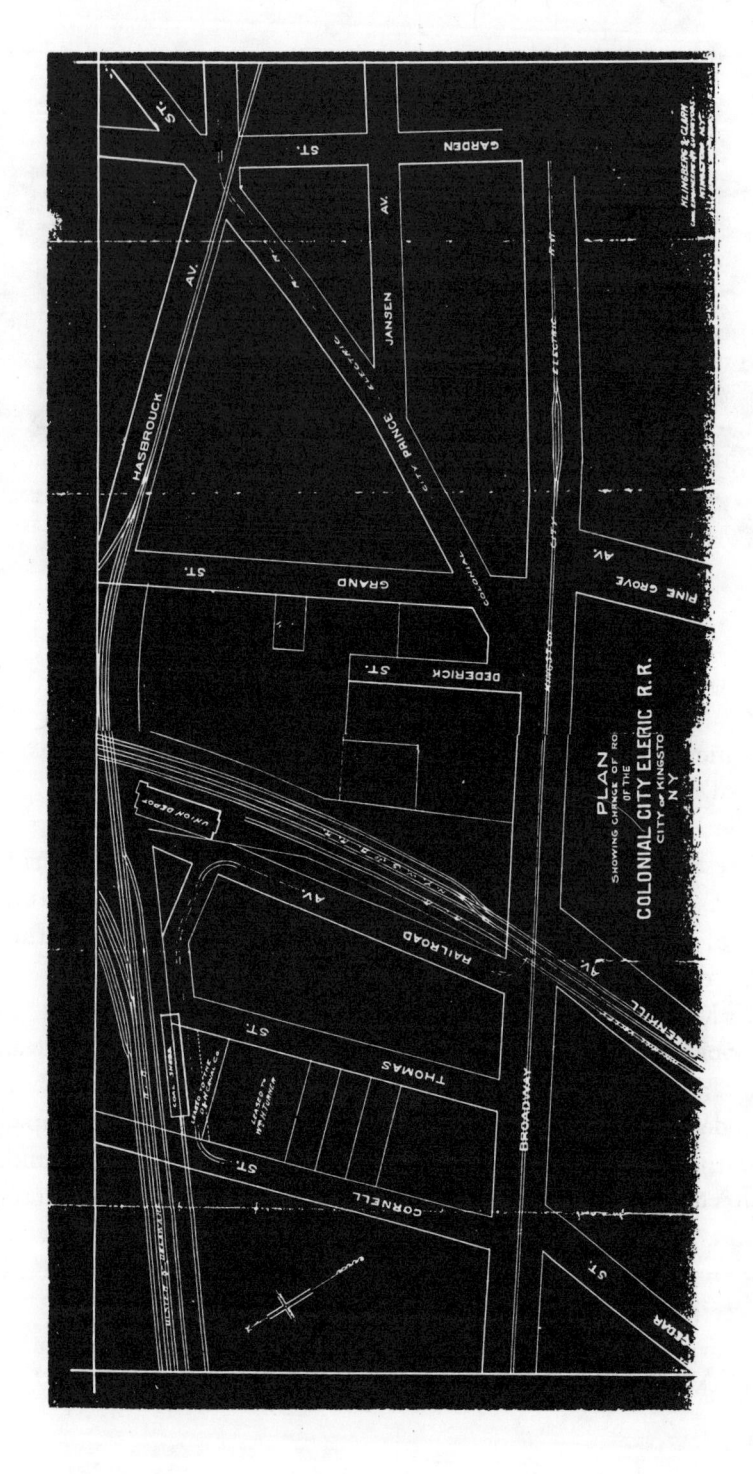

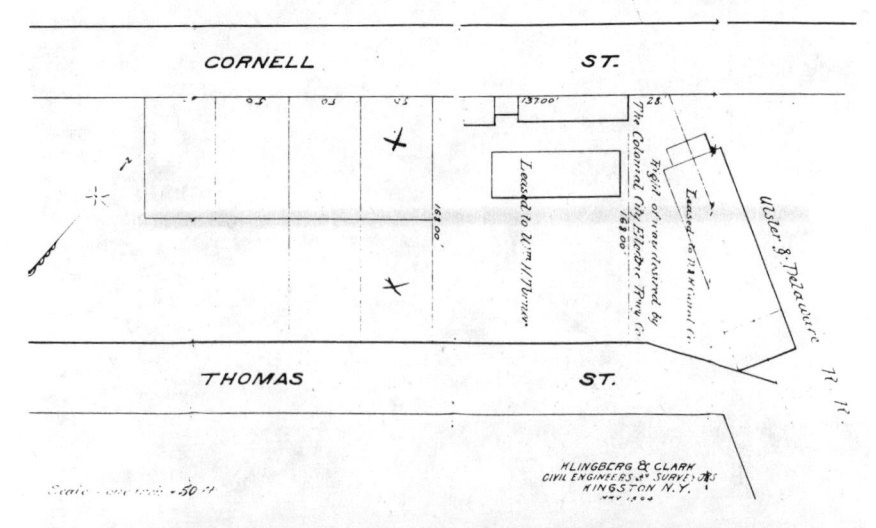

**Above: Right-of-way desired by Colonial City.
Opposite page: Proposed Colonial City route change.**
Courtesy Eugene Dauner

sion of the West Shore Railroad, testified that a total of 14,226 trains passed through Kingston in 1893. C. W. Bradley, superintendent of the West Shore, said that same year the West Shore received 8,070 freight cars from the Ulster & Delaware Railroad and delivered 8,035 cars to the U&D. J. H. Jones also testified about the extensive traffic between the West Shore and the U&D. According to C. Robinson, the West Shore considered the use of a steel viaduct over its tracks to be the best option available. This was confirmed by Charles M. Hilton, a civil engineer for the steam railroad.

William Blood, general superintendent of the Long Island Railroad, addressed the general subject of trolley lines crossing steam railroad lines. Five trolley lines crossed his tracks at grade. He testified that all the crossings involved high risks, and that trolley tracks should either go under or over the railroad's. Joseph Crawford of the Pennsylvania Railroad expressed the same reservations about grade-

**Overleaf, left side: Proposed trestle to cross West Shore tracks.
Overleaf, right side: Proposed trestle to cross U&D tracks.**
Courtesy Eugene Dauner

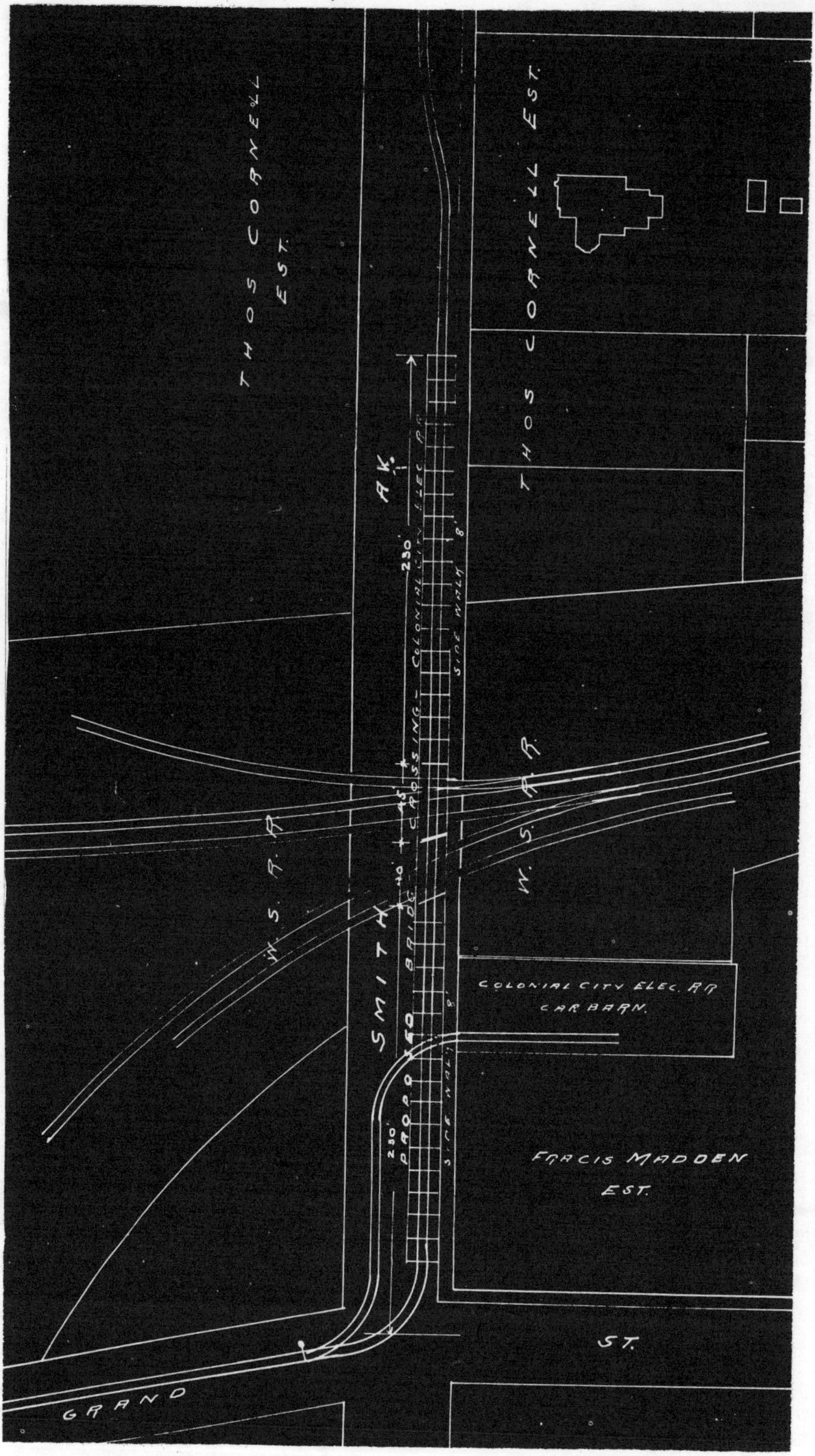
THOS CORNELL EST.
THOS CORNELL EST.
SMITH AV.
PROPOSED BRIDGE CROSSING - COLONIAL CITY ELEC. RR
230'
250'
SIDE WALK 8'
SIDE WALK 8'
W. S. R. R.
W. S. R. R.
COLONIAL CITY ELEC. RR
CAR BARN.
FRACIS MADDEN
EST.
GRAND
ST.

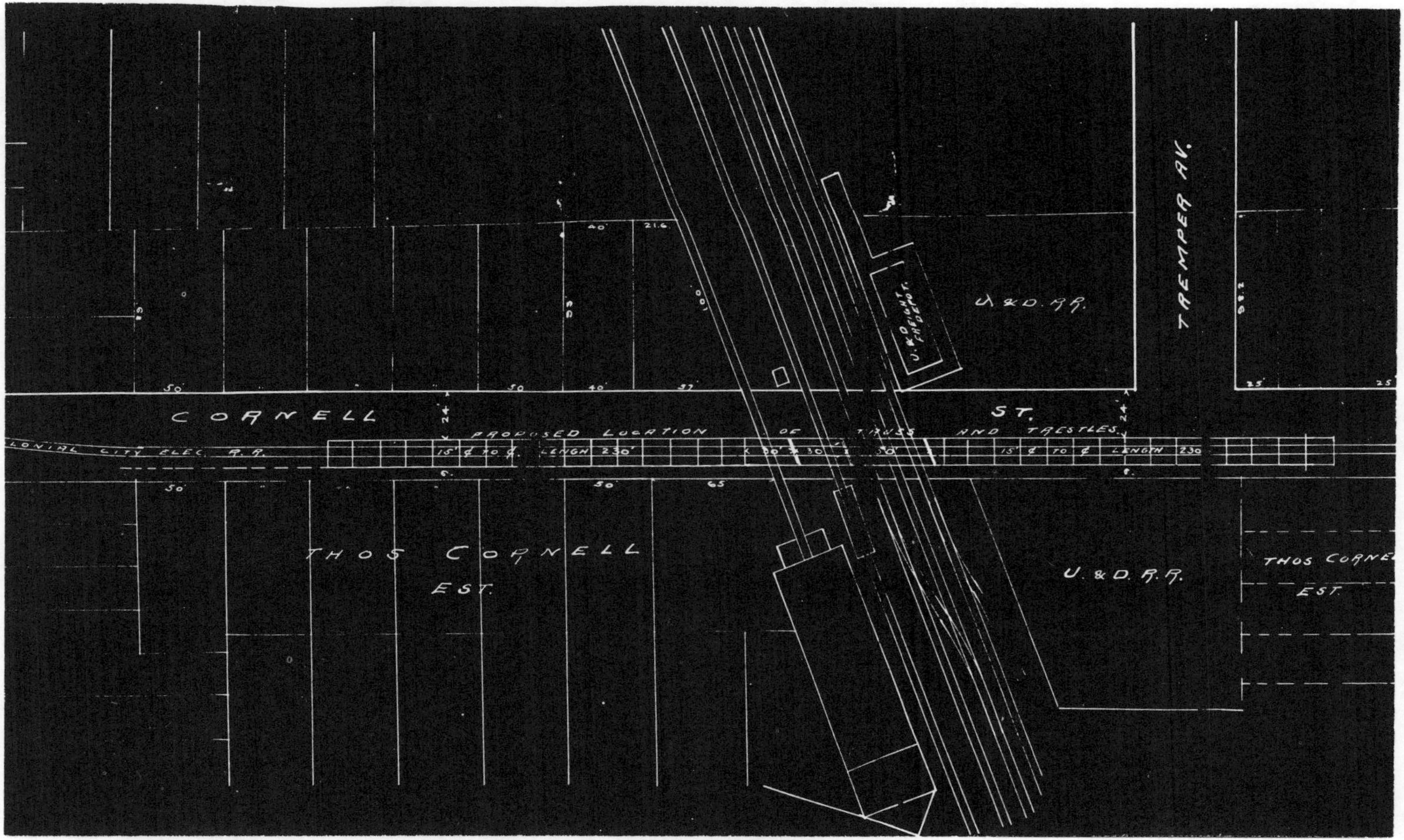
TREMPER AV.
U. & D. R.R.
U. & D. FREIGHT DEPOT.
CORNELL ST.
PROPOSED LOCATION OF TRUSS AND TRESTLES.
15' ¢ TO ¢ LENGH 230'
15' ¢ TO ¢ LENGH 230
COLONIAL CITY ELEC. R.R.
THOS CORNELL EST.
U. & D. R.R.
THOS CORNELL EST.

level crossings, and reiterated the recommendation of Blood. None of the witnesses had any experience with a trolley line crossing five tracks, as would be the case in Kingston. The commission adjourned until May 1 without giving a ruling.

Naturally, Colonial City was left in a quandary. Both sections of its electric line were complete, but unconnected. It could require its passengers to change cars at the West Shore's tracks or set up a temporary detour. On April 20, Colonial applied to the common council to build a temporary pole line. The route would commence at Prince and Hasbrouck Avenue and run through Prince to Broadway and then along Broadway to Cedar, connecting the two sections at this point. After much discussion, the common council agreed. The first week in May, workers started erecting the temporary poles.

On May 10, Colonial City inexplicably requested a postponement on its application to cross the West Shore tracks. A hearing date was set for June 26, then for August 10. Meanwhile, work resumed on the Strand, where the company faced another crossover problem, this time with Ulster & Delaware tracks. U&D officials declared that if Colonial City dared to begin work on a crossover, it would demand a court injunction to prevent the installation.

Sixty men were put to work on the Strand section amid rumors that the company would change its route to avoid confronting the U&D. The rumors suggested that the line would run through private lands from Cornell to Thomas and Railroad Avenue to the West Shore depot. The company said its track would run on Broadway and cars would run to Hasbrouck Avenue by way of Prince Street. A map drawn by the firm of Klingberg & Clark showed these proposed changes and the private lands Colonial City needed to obtain the right-of-way.

The *Leader* reported that Coykendall, of Kingston City, had agreed to this arrangement, but Coykendall, while allowing that his line had agreed to let Colonial City cross its tracks, remained steadfast in his position that Colonial City did not have permission to run on Broadway.

Perhaps because of the continuing trouble with crossings, financial problems arose for Colonial City. N. C. Powelson requested a postponement of the sale of bonds scheduled for June 11 because no one showed up. On July 2, Everett Fowler offered seven first-mortgage bonds worth $1,000 each; he accepted half that amount from Hewitt Boice. On June 18, Goodwin and Swift assigned the trolley line to Arthur E. Walradt in an effort to protect their investment because they were unable to raise money to meet maturing obligations. Work came to a halt, and the financial status of the Colonial City line and Goodwin and Swift became increasingly murky. Campbell and Dempsey owned the car house, and they had a lien on the powerhouse; the franchise for the trolley line belonged to Goodwin and Swift.

Nevertheless, negotiations with the West Shore continued. On July 18, 1894, the parties signed an agreement that Colonial City could bridge the steam tracks if it dropped all suits against the railroad. (See Appendix D.) An undated letter from J. D. Layng, general manager of the West Shore Railroad, to H. G. Young of the Ulster & Delaware purports that the U&D had agreed to a grade-level crossing but that the West Shore would not allow its tracks to be crossed. Colonial City officials must have realized that it would be impossible to cross the steam railroad tracks at grade level. They seemed to be proposing different options to see which would be most acceptable (or the least objectionable) to all parties concerned.

Two days later, Alderman Darling, speaking on behalf of Colonial City, offered a resolution to the common council. This resolution would allow Colonial City to build a temporary trestle on Cornell to cross the Ulster & Delaware tracks, and on Smith Avenue to cross the West Shore tracks. The council finally approved the resolution after considerable discussion.

Property owners on Smith Avenue and Cornell sent a notice to Colonial City objecting to the proposal. They claimed that the trolley line never sought their agreement. They feared that property values would be reduced and noted that, in any case, the company was insolvent. They threatened to take the company to court if it persisted.

On August 25, Judge Parker appointed John E. Kraft of Kingston and Arthur E. Walradt of New York City as receivers of the Colonial

City line. This resulted from a suit initiated by DuBois G. Atkins, who represented Jewell Betty Company, which was trying to collect an overdue bill of $374.31. The reason for appointing receivers was to preclude any creditor from getting undue preference.

While Colonial City floundered, its competitor issued an annual report showing that it owned 2.8 miles of track, carried 929,348 passengers the previous twelve months, and employed twenty-seven. No accidents had occurred during the year. On September 7 it took delivery of two new open cars, each thirty-two feet long, with seating for forty-five passengers. They were manufactured by the Pullman Company and fitted with improved Peckham trucks and the latest General Electric motors. Patrons liked the new cars so much that they would wait for them instead of taking an older car.

In late September, John E. Kraft announced that he hoped to get Colonial City in running condition but offered no plans on how he expected to accomplish this; however, he apparently expected to issue receiver certificates to pay off liens in order to complete the road and obtain rolling stock. Total liabilities amounted to $178,684.35. Judge Parker ordered Goodwin and Swift to deliver to the receivers deeds to the powerhouse and rights-of-way and scheduled a hearing on the issuance of receiver certificates. Kraft and Walradt appeared before him on November 3 seeking the court's permission to issue $35,000 in receiver certificates. The only objection came from Alexander and Green, representing the bond holders. The judge allowed that $27,000 in certificates could be issued but this did not include employee back wages.

In mid-November, Samuel D. Coykendall wrote an open letter to John E. Kraft denying that Kingston City opposed Colonial City crossing its tracks and promising to help his rival when it met the terms of its contract. Another letter claimed that Colonial City had not submitted plans required for either a crossing under or over the steam railroad tracks. However, Coykendall did not want the crossing installed until Colonial City was ready to run. Otherwise, passengers on his line would be subjected to unnecessarily rough crossings.

URBAN TRANSPORTATION IN KINGSTON, NEW YORK, 1866-1930

On December 1, Colonial City requested permission of the common council to change (again) the route of its line. The newly proposed route was to run from Hasbrouck Avenue at the corner of Prince Street, through Prince Street to Dederick, through Dederick to private lands, through private lands across (or beneath, by tunnel) the right-of-way and lands of the West Shore Railroad and Railroad Avenue to private lands, through private lands to Thomas Street, along Thomas Street to Broadway, and along Broadway to Cedar Street. Before it passed the resolution, the common council amended it to state that Colonial City must renew its bond. (See Appendix D for a letter from John E. Kraft to H. G. Young, Cornell estate trustee, requesting consents from the Cornell estate and the Ulster & Delaware Railroad.)

As sections of track were completed, Colonial City began service on the segments that allowed passengers to make connections to the Kingston City line. Car 14 ran from the car barn on Smith Avenue to the end of the line in Ponckhockie on December 7, 1894. It took seven minutes. The motorman on this first trip was C. A. Woolsey employed by General Electric. The car encountered a problem going up Hasbrouck Avenue hill on the return trip and was forced back to Ponckhockie. Regular service commenced using car Number 14 on December 8. Workers lined up the crossover that afternoon so the car could cross the Ulster & Delaware's tracks to the West Shore tracks.

On December 11, a Colonial City car, making its first trip of the day to Ponckhockie, started to go down Hasbrouck Avenue with motorman Chester B. Roe, conductor Costello and one passenger, Charles Schleede, the night watchman at the car barn. A cold rain was falling and freezing on the tracks. When the car reached a point just above the Delaware Avenue bridge, the motorman lost control. The car picked up speed as it rolled along. Passenger Schleede rushed to the platform and jumped. Although he lost his footing when he landed on the frozen ground, he was not badly injured. Conductor Costello ran to the front platform. He and motorman Roe held onto the brake, but the car continued to gain speed. No matter how hard they turned the brake wheel, the car continued to accelerate. When the trolley reached the Ulster & Delaware crossing at Gross' Mill, it bounced into the air but luckily landed back on the track. At this point the trolley tracks started uphill and had been cleared. The locked brakes brought the car to a halt. Surprisingly, no damage had been done.

Colonial City was back in front of the common council on December 28, this time to request permission to tunnel under the West Shore tracks. Coykendall was on hand not to protest the tunneling but rather the common council granting Colonial City permission to run its tracks parallel to those of the Kingston City line on Broadway between Thomas and Cornell Streets. He said that this was a violation of Kingston City's franchise. He also cited a state law that forbade the building of another trolley line parallel to an existing line without permission from the existing line. People on Cornell and Thomas Streets also objected to the petition. They feared a reduction in their property values and problems with drainage caused by the presence of the double tracks. (See Appendix D.) Discussion centered on the intent of Kraft and Colonial City to run beyond the West Shore. However, after all the shouting and objections, the aldermen voted unanimously in favor of the petition.

In a newspaper interview, Coykendall acknowledged that the Kingston City line had obtained an injunction against Colonial City. He pointed out that Kraft had stated at the common council meeting that he wanted to settle the issue of whether Kingston City had exclusive rights to run its line on Broadway. Coykendall told the reporter that now Kraft had his "chance to fight it out in court." Coykendall boasted that his line had never objected to the franchise of Colonial City or to the many changes it requested from the common council, but questioned the management ability of John E. Kraft. On January 2, 1895, an injunction was granted by Judge Herrick and served on receiver Kraft et al. The injunction forbade Colonial City from constructing, extending or operating its cars on Broadway between Cornell and Thomas Streets.

The first serious accident on the Kingston City line occurred at 10:30 A.M. on January 7, 1895, when car Number 1 was coming down Broadway hill. The car had on board Mrs. James Seifferth, her sister

Urban Transportation in Kingston, New York, 1866-1930

Kate Mulligan, Dr. Thomas P. Ostrander, Hiram Best, his son Harry, a man and a boy from Germantown, conductor James Norton and motorman Charles Link. Shortly before the car reached the switch near St. Mary's Church, it began to rain and the rails became coated with ice. Seifferth and Mulligan were going to St. Mary's, and they asked the conductor to let them off at the switch, but the motorman was unable to stop the car due to the ice. It continued downhill, gathering momentum. Link applied the front brakes and Norton the rear brakes, without success. Dr. Ostrander jumped from the rear platform and rolled a considerable distance. The conductor prevented others from jumping. Witnesses estimated that the car reached ninety miles per hour near Spring Street. It continued down the hill until it reached Ferry Street. Just before the car left the tracks, Best and his son jumped. With Link still at his post, it traveled twenty-five feet before breaking an iron pillar and crashing part way into the Cornell Steamboat Company office, where it damaged windows, woodwork and radiators and sustained considerable damage (the front platform was broken off and the truck bent). Motorman Link, unconscious with a fractured skull, was taken to Kingston Hospital. The others aboard suffered from shock but received no serious injuries. Doctors Stern, Chambers, VanHoovenbergh, Norwood and Munn removed a piece of bone from Link's skull. Link regained consciousness shortly after the operation. He was released from the hospital on January 27 and later sued the Kingston City line for $25,000, and eventually settled for $10,000.

The same freezing rain caused a Colonial City car to slide as it came down Hasbrouck Avenue with motorman Valsh and conductor Murphy and no passengers. Again the brakes proved useless as the car gained speed; it crossed the Ulster & Delaware tracks at Murray Street and was saved by an upgrade just beyond.

Troubles continued for Colonial City as four men who worked in the powerhouse quit over a salary dispute. They were Frank Brown, chief engineer; Theodore Boice, electrician; and J. Herbert and Frank Cramer, firemen. At the time the line went into receivership, Walradt promised to pay these men, a promise that was honored until about December 8, when they were asked by Wilgott Klingberg, a Colonial City engineer, to accept their pay monthly instead of weekly. When the workers refused, their pay interval became irregular. A promise of full pay failed to keep the men on the job, and replacements were hired: Milton Bell, engineer, and Michael Sullivan and Frank Lusk, firemen. When the four replaced workers appeared at the company office demanding their back pay, an altercation ensued. Klingerg hit Boice while trying to eject him from the building and a fist fight developed. (Appendix E contains the Receiver's Financial Report.)

On January 14, Judge Herrick held a hearing on the continuation of the injunction. Judge Clearwater presented the case on behalf of the Kingston City line and J. N. Fiero and Alva S. Newcomb represented Colonial City. They argued that the judge should have issued the injunction against the company instead of against Kraft and Walradt. Therefore, Judge Herrick let the injunction stand against Colonial City but not against the receivers, but he ruled that Kingston City, if it wished, could require the receivers to appear at the next hearing. Although the injunction continued, Colonial City placed ties on Prince Street and on Dederick Street.

Meanwhile, former powerhouse employees Frank Brown and J. Herbert Cramer retained Eckert and Westbrook to collect their claims against Colonial City. Cramer claimed the company owed him $99 for work he had done, and Brown claimed the company owed him $112.50. In addition, Brown claimed that Walradt owed him $130 as assign for Goodwin and Swift. Likewise, Cramer claimed Walradt owed him $81.

On February 5, Judge Parker, after listening to all the arguments of both trolley lines and accepting all the documents prepared by both sides, vacated the injunction against Colonial City, and the line began operating again. Judge Clearwater told a *Freeman* reporter that the Kingston City Railroad would not appeal Judge Parker's decision. (See Appendix F.)

Before March came, both lines had to grapple with heavy snow and breakdowns. Kingston City repaired car Number 1 and returned it to service. Colonial City car Number 12 collided with a carriage containing four ladies returning from a funeral; there were no injuries. Then the common council proposed an ordinance defining the maximum speeds of trolley cars where they crossed each other's and the steam railroad's tracks. The lines argued that the council was treading on the jurisdiction of the railroad commission, which subsequently considered the matter on March 21 and ruled that the speed of all cars be reduced to four miles per hour at all trolley crossings; that when cars having the right-of-way were within seventy-five feet of the crossing, they had the right to proceed and that cars not having the right-of-way must come to a stop within twenty-five feet of the crossing and must not proceed until the other car had passed.

By March 23, the Mercantile Trust Company had begun foreclosure action against the Colonial City Electric Railway Company and others, covering all the property of the railroad, real estate, tracks, machinery, cars, equipment, etc. The sale under foreclosure would wipe out the receivership.

In spite of the foreclosure proceedings, labor unrest due to deferred payrolls, and numerous breakdowns caused by such things as limbs falling across and breaking electric lines, Colonial City went ahead adding car Number 12, a vestibuled car built by the St. Louis car company with Diamond trucks, and began work on the Thomas Street extension. A stockholder told reporters that work on the proposed tunnel would begin shortly. Workers laid track and installed wire to Railroad Avenue. Colonial City expected that cars would run to the depot on the uptown section.

The first fatal accident involving a trolley car in Kingston occurred on April 28, 1895. A Colonial City car was proceeding down Hasbrouck Avenue near Gross' mill pond when three-year-old Harry Klein tried to cross the tracks. The motorman, Francis Boyle, was unable to stop the car in time. He ran the car to the first switch and stopped. Then he and his conductor, William Mellert, went to city hall and turned themselves in. They were released on $1,000 bail pending the outcome of the coroner's inquest.

In April, Kingston City ordered some new open cars from the Pullman Car Company. These were to use trucks built and installed by the Peckham Truck and Car Wheel Company of Kingston. Delivery took place in May. That month, during a heavy thunder shower, lightning hit a trolley wire. The electric charge ran along the wire and down the trolley pole of Kingston City's open car Number 8 on Fair Street. The charge exploded the rear motor, making a sound like a cannon being fired. No other damage was done, but the passengers were badly frightened. The same charge slightly damaged car Number 5.

The foreclosure action against Colonial City moved slowly as T. B. Westbrook, the referee in the proceeding, tried to establish a method of transferring the receivers' accounts. Employees were due back wages and Colonial City's annual report showed a loss of $9,482 for its fiscal year. The company paid general officers and clerks $1,434 and other employees $7,978; fuel cost $1,982 and insurance $296.

In mid-November, Judge Parker granted a judgment of foreclosure for the Mercantile Trust Company against the Colonial City Electric Railroad Company. The amount due on the mortgage was approximately $170,000 for principal and interest. By order of the judge, the minimum amount acceptable to purchase Colonial City was $70,000, which would cover the expenses of foreclosure and the receivers' indebtedness and fund of $10,000, held as security pending the action of Reed and McKibben. The judge appointed John T. Cloonan referee to sell the property. Cloonan set December 12 as the day of sale.

When the sale day came, Cloonan sold the company to Charles Stewart, representing the bondholders' committee comprising August Belmont, John I. Waterbury and Charles M. Preston. Stewart's bid of $70,000 was the only one. Plans were made to reorganize and complete the road. In the interim, receivers ran the company.

Early in January 1896, the Colonial City Traction Company filed articles of incorporation with the New York Secretary of State and the Ulster County Clerk. The incorporators were Charles M. Preston, John I. Waterbury, August Belmont, John E. Kraft, William F. Russell, William Hutton, Abram Hasbrouck, Gilbert D. B. Hasbrouck, George Hutton, Hewitt Boice, Otis M. Preston, Guilford Hasbrouck, Conrad E. Hasbrouck, Reuben Bernard and George S. Sleight. (See Appendix G.) The board of directors of the new company held a meeting in New York City to define its organization.

January 18 was fixed as the date for closing the accounts of the receivers.

Judge Parker heard the accounting of the receivers. Since there was no opposition, he approved the accounting, and the receivers were allowed to divide $3,500 for their work. The St. Louis Car Company, represented by S. B. Sharpe, alleged that Colonial City had not paid for three cars, but the judge disallowed this claim. Charles M. Preston, president of the new company, represented Colonial City Traction at the hearing. A week later, Sharpe again requested that a sufficient sum be set aside for three trolley cars and six trucks his company had sold to Colonial City. After receiving statements from both parties, the judge ordered $6,500 set aside for security of the St. Louis Car Company, and he closed the receivership.

The new board authorized Preston to run the company. Charles H. Ledlie, an able railroad man from St. Louis, was elected as superintendent. He replaced W. Klingberg, who was superintendent under the receivers. The company located its office in the Hasbrouck row on the Strand. Hasbrouck Alliger was appointed bookkeeper, and the company designated the National Bank of Rondout as its depository. Most important for the public, the company announced a new schedule: A car would leave from the West Shore Railroad station in both directions at 5:30 A.M. (7:00 A.M. on Sunday) and from Ponckhockie and Linderman Avenue before 6:00 A.M. (7:15 A.M. on Sunday). This schedule guaranteed connections with the 6:25 A.M. West Shore train.

In mid-March the Colonial City Traction Company appeared before the Kingston Common Council to request permission to extend its line to Kingston Point and to run on Broadway from Cedar to Prince Streets. Gilbert D. B. Hasbrouck, representing Colonial Traction, stated that there were no objections to extending the line to Kingston Point. He further claimed that under the law Colonial Traction could put up to 1,500 feet of track next to Kingston City's track on Broadway. He also declared that his company could not cross Railroad Avenue because the Cornell estate owned the property. His rival, Samuel Coykendall, objected, saying the common council did not have the authority to grant permission to Colonial Traction to put track on Broadway. He pointed out that Colonial had previously said it wanted to use Kingston City tracks, but the present resolution called for laying new track. He also observed that two sets of trolley tracks would cause more problems at the West Shore crossing. His company planned to institute five-minute service starting May 1. Allowing Colonial Traction to use Kingston City track on Broadway would make this proposed schedule impossible to keep, he said. Besides, had not Colonial asked the common council for permission to institute several different solutions for connecting its two sections? Even when granted permission to build a tunnel, Colonial never followed through. Coykendall said he believed that Colonial Traction had no intention to run on Broadway and its request was a ploy to get his line to buy out its competitor.

About two weeks later, Colonial Traction presented an application to Judge Parker for the appointment of commissioners to assess damages for using Kingston City line tracks on Broadway between Prince and Cedar Streets. Hasbrouck again represented Colonial; Clearwater represented Kingston City. Clearwater made a motion to dismiss the petition because facts had not been provided to prove that Judge Parker's court had jurisdiction in the matter, and because

Kingston City Trolley----shuttle to the West Shore station.
From DeLisser, *Picturesque Ulster*

Colonial Traction did not have the consent of the common council nor of adjacent property owners. Further, he alleged that Colonial was not properly incorporated and had not complied with state laws concerning street-surface railroads. He pointed to safety concerns and potential loss of business.

The hearing continued in late May. Witnesses for both sides testified as to the ease or difficulty of joint usage of the track in question. The hearing was adjourned to mid-July. In the meantime, Colonial City Traction obtained a temporary injunction from Judge Joseph F. Barnard of Poughkeepsie restraining Kingston City from running its cars over that portion of the Strand where Colonial Traction cars ran. Kingston City proposed operating cars over Ulster & Delaware tracks from the junction of Ferry Street and the Strand to Kingston Point. It would not allow people riding the Colonial City Traction line to its terminus in Ponckhockie to walk to Kingston Point over the railroad trestle. It appeared that the point involved was the same one in question on Broadway.

Before Judge Parker's court reconvened, Russell, Belmont and Waterbury resigned as directors of Colonial Traction. The remaining directors elected Alva S. Newcomb in William F. Russell's place and left the other places vacant. The common council demanded paving between the tracks, but this apparently could be stalled with promises until the company showed a profit.

In Judge Parker's court the battle over Broadway continued. Coykendall offered to get Colonial Traction the right to tunnel under Railroad Avenue and the West Shore tracks from its terminus on its eastern division in order to connect with the other end on Dederick Street. He offered to present a bond for $50,000 to guarantee obtaining the necessary consents from the various interests, including the Cornell estate, and to pay the estate any sum more than $2,000 awarded as damages by commissioners named by Judge Parker. Preston and Hasbrouck rejected the offer as too indefinite. The judge then removed the temporary injunction against Kingston City because Samuel D. Coykendall and George Coykendall d said they never intended to extend their line beyond its present terminus. It appeared to him that Colonial City Traction did not want Kingston

City to run parallel to its tracks on the Strand any more than Kingston City wanted Colonial to run parallel to its line on Broadway, and on August 10, he granted the application for the appointment of commissioners to fix damages for the use of Kingston City tracks on Broadway. The commissioners appointed by the court were William L. Learned, Campbell W. Adams and Elnathan Sweet. Kingston City appealed the decision.

The first week in August, Kingston City put a spur from its tracks on Broadway to Union Depot. This enterprise was kept secret. The West Shore Railroad allowed the tracks to cross the lawn of the depot. On Sunday morning, just past midnight, a crew of 200 laid the spur. Even rain did not stop the work.

On October 2, the common council considered the Kingston City line's application to extend its tracks from the junction of East Union Street through private lands to the Ulster & Delaware Railroad. The line had filed this application on September 8. Alderman Powers offered an ordinance granting the application. At this point, John E. Kraft, secretary of Colonial City Traction, said he did not oppose the application except that his company had also applied to run over North Street. The common council had denied a previous application, and the mayor vetoed the second application. However, Preston had no objection to Kingston City's application as long as the council allowed Colonial to run on North Street also. Alderman Tammany offered an amendment to grant both applications. The mayor declared his motion out of order, and the council passed Powers' ordinance.

Next, the council took up the Colonial Traction application. Coykendall opposed it, stating that his company already had a franchise to operate on North Street and, once again, that the common council did not have the power to grant two franchises on the same street. The council defeated Colonial's application.

Late in October, Colonial Traction hired Peter Measter to build an eighty-foot by twenty-four-foot car barn at its Railroad Avenue terminus. Shortly after it was finished, Oliver A. Perrine boarded car Number 8. He remained on the steps of the car while it was passing through the barn, but he was caught in the narrow space between the car and the wall and badly injured.

By late November, Kingston City had laid rails through North Street from the Strand to Delaware Avenue, using regular steam railroad rails. The company received the first of its big new cars from the Pullman Palace Car Company. The new car had double doors, wide aisles and seats upholstered in blue.

On November 18, the common council granted the Ulster & Delaware permission to construct and maintain an additional track across the Strand to simplify switching, but with the proviso that its street committee and the city engineer supervise the construction. The railroad did nothing to install the crossing until mid-December when, shortly after midnight, a gang of men started laying railroad track across the track of the Colonial City Traction Company. This unconnected track crossed the Strand and Colonial's tracks diagonally. It is not clear whether the street committee or city engineer was present, as Coykendall alleged in a letter to the mayor. (See Appendix D.)

The following night, a group of men, apparently working for Colonial, tore up the crossing unhindered. In a letter to the mayor, Coykendall claimed that the city was responsible for any damage incurred by the removal of U&D tracks. Colonial Traction countered that the common council had no right to grant the Ulster & Delaware permission to cross Colonial's tracks without its consent. This was the same argument Coykendall used when Colonial wished to cross his tracks.

A confrontation at the site seemed unavoidable. The next night at 12:30 A.M. a gang of fifty U&D trackmen began removing macadam from outside Colonial's tracks at the crossing. Apparently expecting trouble, the trolley line had a car running back and forth over the crossing. Police Chief Hood and seven policemen appeared and ordered the car to stop. Motorman Balch refused, and Hood arrested him, cut the rope connecting the trolley to its power and moved the car from the crossing. Next, the U&D ran an engine with an attached car over Colonial's tracks to prevent any other trolley cars from approaching. Then the track gang, under the direction of

Chief Hood, laid down the crossing. Balch was released on bail. Hood told reporters he acted under orders from Mayor Weiber. City Engineer Klingberg denied he had been present when the first crossing was laid.

The battle of the crossing escalated. Around 3:30 the following afternoon, a gang of fifteen to twenty Colonial Traction men started to remove the crossing when Ulster & Delaware officials learned of their action and dispatched an engine and five flatcars loaded with stone to the crossing. A Colonial trolley car on the track was smashed to pieces by the train. The impact knocked the rear flatcar from the U&D track onto the Colonial track, where it hit a wagon. Because Colonial had a car on the Ponckhockie side, passengers could ride to the wreck, walk around it and board a car on the opposite side to finish their trip.

A large crowd gathered quickly. Police refused requests by Colonial officials to clear the street, move the train and arrest the engineer. Alderman John F. Irwin tried to intervene but was rebuffed by the engineer and the police. Police reinforcements arrived and, finally, U&D officials ordered the train removed from the crossing. No sooner was this done than Colonial Traction men returned to their shovel work. Ulster & Delaware men shoveled right back. Emotions were running high and a riot seemed possible. Both sides appealed to Undersheriff DuMond, but he said he could do nothing until an actual disturbance occurred. U&D and Colonial officials conferred in the street and later in the U&D offices (Coykendall was in New York City at the time), but no compromise could be reached, and the standoff continued until evening, when the railroad brought in two carloads of men prepared to protect the crossing, or put it back in if necessary, and Colonial learned that its men would be arrested if they tried to remove the crossing. In the meantime, Klingberg changed his story, stating that he approved the crossing and was present at its installation in accordance with the common council resolution.

Friends of George Balch filled the courtroom when he came to trial before Kingston City Recorder Murray, who repeatedly denied requests by Balch's attorney to dismiss the charges or turn the case over to a justice of the peace or impanel a jury. At last the recorder agreed to send the case to the grand jury in January and left Balch free on $500 bail. (No record was found as to the disposition of Balch's case.)

In mid-December, the Board of Police Commissioners held a special meeting at a late hour in Mayor Weiber's store to create a special force of twenty-one officers to help if any more disturbances occurred. Not surprisingly, all of the special officers named were either Ulster & Delaware employees, employees of other Coykendall corporations, or Coykendall sympathizers. (See Appendix H.) The injunction obtained by the U&D restraining Colonial City Traction from removing the crossover on the Strand was set aside by Judge Parker on December 19.

The City of Kingston, represented by Corporation Counsel Cloonan, appeared before Judge Barnard in Poughkeepsie on January 2, 1897, asking for a continuance of the injunction against the Ulster & Delaware, represented by Judge Clearwater. Gilbert D. B. Hasbrouck presented the Colonial City Traction Company. Clearwater argued that the U&D had the right to make the crossover based on the resolution of the common council and of certain old grants to the U&D's predecessor, the Rondout & Oswego, by the former Village of Rondout. He asked the court to continue the injunction against the Colonial line and to drop the one against the U&D. Hasbrouck maintained that there was collusion between the city authorities and the U&D. Further, he said that the land on which Colonial's track was placed belonged to it and no one else could use the land without Colonial's consent. Hasbrouck also alluded to Judge Parker's decision vacating the injunction. After hearing the arguments from all sides, Judge Barnard continued the injunction and instructed all parties to take the matter to court and resolve the issues without any more disturbance on the street.

Because Colonial Traction had not obtained the common council's approval to use Kingston City's track on Broadway, the appellate court reversed Judge Parker's decision to appoint commissioners to ascertain damages due Kingston City. Colonial did not give up, and the battle over Broadway moved back to the common council and up to Albany. In Albany, an amendment to Section 102 of railroad law relating to the use of another line's track (which would have thwarted Colonial's plan entirely) passed the legislature but was vetoed by the governor. In Kingston, the common council again heard arguments from the rivals. Colonial pleaded for the prerequisite council approval, the judicial system needed to resolve the issue. The approval was granted but vetoed by the mayor; the council overrode his veto.

Late in May, Kingston City ran its first car to Kingston Point. It used the Ulster & Delaware track as far as Turck's Mill in Ponckhockie, and then ran from these on new track. When service began, motormen discovered large pieces of timber across the track. The perpetrators were never discovered.

In early June, the appellate court vacated the injunction obtained by the City of Kingston against Colonial City Traction and the Ulster & Delaware. The judges ruled that the U&D did not have the right to cross over Colonial's track without its permission, nor to obtain the right through condemnation proceedings. The judges also ruled that the City of Kingston had the power and authority to remove any obstacles from the streets without an injunction.

Apparently the Ulster & Delaware wanted to use its tracks on the Strand to operate an electric trolley, for shortly after the injunction was removed, Colonial was back in court seeking an injunction to prevent the U&D from operating a street railway, but Judge Barnard ruled that it was within the rights of the railroad to use its tracks as it saw fit, with or without electricity. The perils of running the rival lines close together was brought home in late July when a summer storm caused a wire used by the U&D to fall across the wires of Colonial Traction at the intersection of the Strand and Ferry Street. A large crowd gathered to watch as sparks sizzled and sputtered.

Finally, desperate to connect its two sections while its case languished, Colonial started using a stage, painted yellow and blue like its trolley cars. The stagecoach was low slung, making it easy for passengers to get in and out as they were transferred from one section to the other.

On September 29, 1897, at 10:30 P.M., a West Shore locomotive crashed into a Kingston City trolley car at the Broadway crossing. Apparently the West Shore's gateman was tardy in lowering the gate, and for this he lost his job. Quick braking by the trolley's motorman saved his passengers and all but the front end of the trolley.

Throughout the fall and winter of 1897 the two sides maneuvered for position in the continuing fight over Broadway. In the first week of October, the Court of Appeals handed down a judgment against Colonial Traction's use of Kingston City's tracks on Broadway. Did this supersede the permission granted by the common council? Colonial did not think so. Kingston City changed its tactics and purchased exclusive rights from seven adjacent property owners "to build, maintain and operate a street railroad upon Broadway, along and in front of the premises of the parties named." The conveyances also revoked any prior consents. Meanwhile, the railroad commission continued to hold hearings.

Just when it looked as if Kingston's great trolley war would drag on into the twentieth century, rumors began circulating that Colonial City Traction would build a tunnel under Kingston City's spur, under the West Shore tracks and under Railroad Avenue. They were true. Samuel D. Coykendall gave his consent to build the tunnel under his spur and the land of the Cornell estate. The West Shore gave its blessing and granted the trolley line permission to build a storm sewer with an outlet in Jacob's Valley to drain the tunnel. Colonial purchased or already controlled the balance of the rights necessary, including the approach to the tunnel. Municipal consent had been secured during the receivership. While Colonial mulled over its subway plan, it received word that the commissioners had concluded their hearings and approved Colonial's use of Kingston City's Broadway track. They conveyed their decision to the Appellate Division of the Supreme Court, but the tunnel idea was gaining momentum, and by mid-July bids had been solicited that varied from $25,723.55 to $36,213.00. Just after the bids were opened, a special delivery letter arrived from Reading, Pennsylvania, with a bid of $22,745.25, and on August 6, stockholders approved this low bid by Samuel W. Frescoln. Plans called for the tunnel to be thirteen feet

UPTOWN—DOWNTOWN; HORSECARS—TROLLEY CARS

Above: Broadway railroad crossing.

Left: Trolley car in front of the Fair Street Opera House.

Below: Trolley hit by West Shore train at the Broadway crossing.

Courtesy The Trolley Museum of New York

wide and eighteen feet deep at its lowest point. (See Appendices I and J.)

The contractor was given sixty days to complete the tunnel. An interesting clause in the contract gave local people preference for employment. J. Curtis and J. J. Callagne of the Frescoln Company arrived about ten days after the awarding of the contract, and a week later work started at Dederick Street. On September 17, Colonial Traction extended its track on Thomas Street to Railroad Avenue between the Hotel Eichler and Bauer's Hotel and directly opposite the West Shore Depot. Fifty men labored to lay the 520 feet of track and complete the overhead wiring in one day, and by evening a car operated by Chester B. Roe and B. J. Murray ran over the new section amid the cheers of onlookers.

By November, Colonial had extended its line to the intersection of Prince Street, Dederick Street and Broadway and around into Dederick Street to the entrance of the new subway. On December 16, workers tunneled through. Joseph Boyd of the West Shore Railroad was the first person to walk through the tunnel, which was dug from both ends and met under the West Shore's tracks. Masonry and steel work continued through the winter.

On March 20, 1899, the first car went through the new Colonial City subway shortly after 5:00 P.M. Passengers included Mayor Brinnier and several other prominent men and officials of the road. At last, the tunnel allowed the connection of the line's two sections.

With its passengers in mind, Colonial completed a handsome stone walk from the top steps at the subway's entrance to the depot, painted the interior walls of the subway white, covered the overhead at the station with heavy glass and added cushioned seats for patrons awaiting a trolley car. Six new open cars mounted on Diamond trucks were bought from the Jackson and Sharpe Company of Wilmington, Delaware. Six closed cars ("latest style") were added in August.

Patronage of both lines was heavy throughout the 1890s. On July 4, 1898, Kingston City reported carrying 20,000 passengers and on Decoration Day (now Memorial Day), 17,000. Cars were rented for social events. For example, the Rondout Social Mannerchor chartered a trolley car to run over the entire Colonial line, with a stop

UPTOWN—DOWNTOWN; HORSECARS—TROLLEY CARS

Colonial City subway under the West Shore tracks looking south.
Courtesy The Trolley Museum of New York

for songs and refreshments at Frederick Leudthe's house on Washington Avenue, the same night, a Miss Myers of Clinton Avenue had a trolley party, treating her friends to a ride over the entire line.

As the century drew to a close, the lines competed in more decorous ways: Kingston City added new Pullman Company cars with cane seats on each side of a middle aisle. Colonial announced it would run cars every ten minutes until 10:00 P.M. and every twenty minutes until midnight. When its superintendent resigned to take and engineering job in St. Louis, Colonial employees presented him with a gold-mounted silk umbrella.

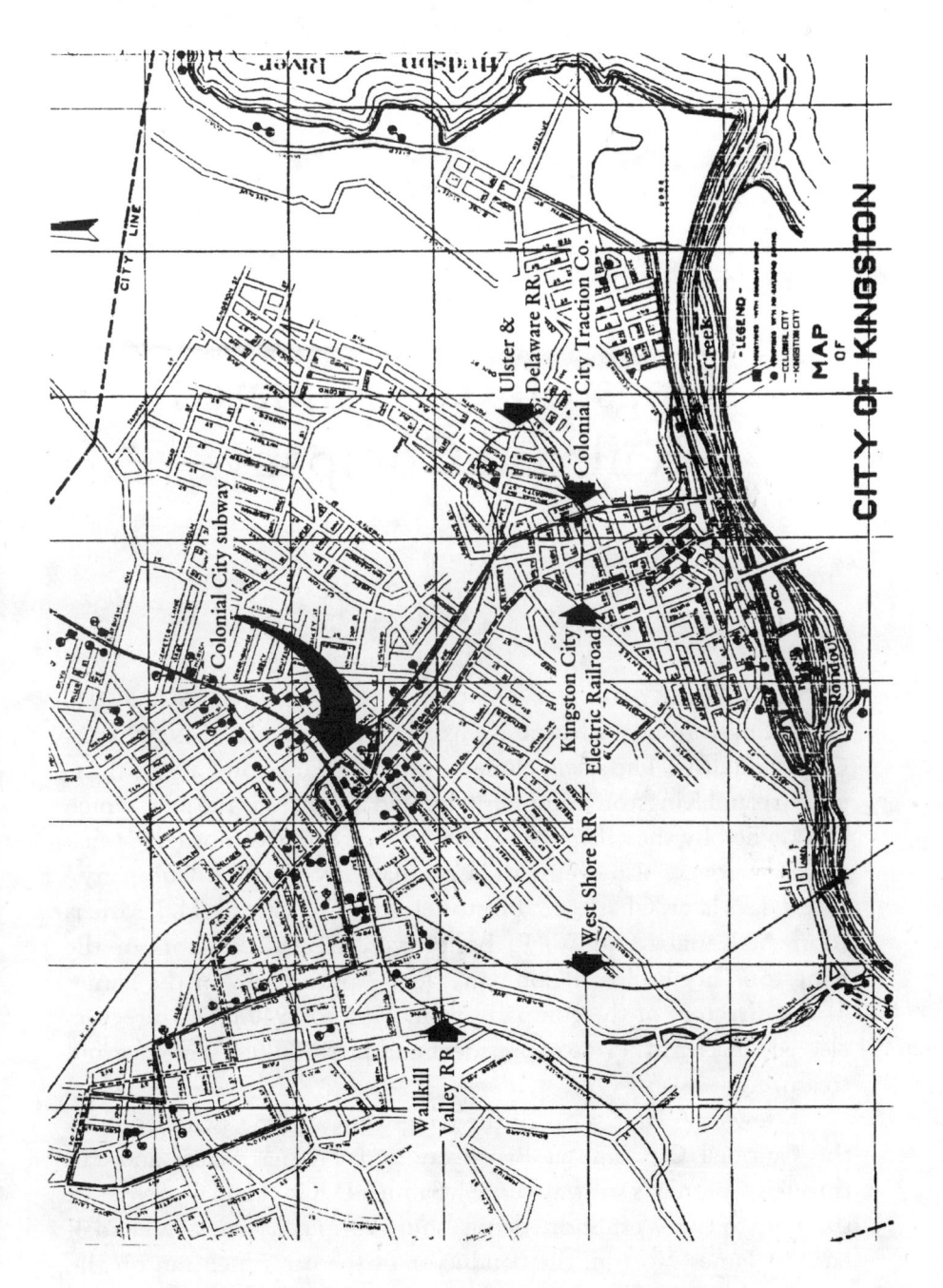

URBAN TRANSPORTATION IN KINGSTON, NEW YORK, 1866-1930

Kingston's trolley lines, railroads, and subway.
Courtesy The Trolley Museum of New York (map modified by the author)

Kingston Consolidated Railroad Company

ON JANUARY 17, 1901, SAMUEL D. COYKENDALL SOLD THE Kingston City Electric Railroad to a syndicate of New York City capitalists. The sale included the entire Kingston City line, the car barn and Kingston Point Park, but did not include the pier, which was owned by the Ulster & Delaware Railroad. (Rumor had it that the buyers were also eyeing the Colonial City Traction Company.) A few days later, Charles M. Preston, John I. Waterbury, H. J. Miller, John A. Kenney and W. P. Bolles were elected directors of the Kingston City Railroad Company. (See Appendix K for the names of the directors of the company from 1905 to 1910.) The directors elected Charles M. Preston president and J. A. Kenney secretary and treasurer.

A few days later, a car of the Kingston City line switched onto the Colonial City line at Broadway and Thomas Street and ran through Colonial's subway tunnel. Samuel D. Coykendall, owner of the spur to the West Shore depot, shut the spur down. Coykendall laid off James Norton, the conductor of the car which ran on the spur, and Hiram Holmes, the motorman. Norton had worked for the Kingston City line for 25 years.

By the end of January 1901, the New York City group had acquired both the Kingston City and the Colonial City lines. These were operated separately under the parent company, named the Kingston Consolidated Railroad Company. At the same time, the management of the Kingston City line appointed William B. Taylor general manager, replacing Abram Hasbrouck, who was acting superintendent. Taylor had been superintendent of the North Jersey Street Railroad in Jersey City, New Jersey. In mid-July, at a meeting of the Kingston Consolidated Railroad Company, C. Gordon Reel, of St. Louis, Missouri, was elected a director and vice president of the company. He was given general charge and supervision over the road, though Taylor continued as general manager.

In the summer, the Kingston City cars left from Marius Street every ten minutes until 10:15 p.m. and from Kingston Point every ten minutes until 10:45 p.m. In September, the Kingston City cars ran only as far as the Kingston-Rhinecliff ferry. Cars on the Colonial City division ran to Kingston Point. In early October, a petition to the common council from residents and taxpayers along the Colonial City line asked that Colonial City run its cars every ten minutes, according to its charter. The common council referred the petition to the corporation counsel and to the railroad committee. Two days later, Kingston Consolidated announced the Colonial City division would run a ten-minute schedule from 8:00 a.m. to 9:00 p.m. from Marius Street to Kingston Point, and the Kingston City division would operate from the head of Wall Street to the Kingston-Rhinecliff ferry. The company's commitment to its schedules seems to be sincere: Late in February 1902, a snowstorm lasting thirty-four hours hit the region. Kingston Consolidated kept the cars running on time.

In early March 1902, Kingston Consolidated enlarged and improved the powerhouse in Ponckhockie. New boilers and dynamos enabled the company to produce more power from the facility.

In November, a new city sewer line was begun on Prince Street, which forced the Kingston City division to alter its routes and schedules to run from Marius Street to East Union Street on a ten-minute schedule. The Colonial City division ran from Wall and North Front Streets to the ferry on a twenty-minute schedule. These routes and schedules remained in effect until the sewer project was completed.

On January 21, 1903, motorman Dick Murphy and conductor Charles Murphy were on duty on Broadway hill, running vestibule car Number 9 to keep the track open. Late that night, ice had formed on the track near St. Mary's Church, and the car, descending the hill, could not be stopped. At Abeel Street, Charles Murphy jumped; Dick Murphy stuck to his post. At Ferry Street, the car jumped the track and crashed about five feet into the front of the Cornell Building, wrecking the car and the entire front of the office of the Cornell Towing Company. Dick Murphy, unconscious, was knocked backward and covered with glass. Hundreds of people later came to see the wreck and to watch the trolley towed back to the car barn.

Another severe snowstorm hit Kingston on November 13, 1904. The storm broke the trolley wires at the corner of Main and Fair Streets, and by 9:00 p.m. so many wires were down that the power-

Trolley car #9 after crashing into Cornell Building, 1903.
Courtesy of Joseph Fautz

house was shut down to prevent shorts caused by other electric lines falling on the trolley wires. The Colonial City division shut down at 7:00 p.m. An all-night effort allowed resumption of travel on the two divisions by morning.

Kingston Consolidated snowplow in 1900s.
Courtesy The Trolley Museum of New York

Early in January 1905, snow again visited Kingston, and again work cars kept running all night to keep the tracks open. In addition, a sand wagon was kept busy on both Hasbrouck Avenue and Broadway hill. (See Appendix L for Kingston Consolidated Railroad rule book.) Even so, cars on the Colonial City division could not make it up Hasbrouck Avenue. C. Gordon Reel and a crew of five men used his patented snowplow to clear the line, first plowing about twenty feet, backing the plow down and attacking again. By afternoon the route was open.

On June 2, 1905, the common council street committee notified Kingston Consolidated to stop work on its track on Broadway near Delaware Avenue, where the company was installing T-rail. Alderman McCullough introduced a resolution to investigate the use of T-rail, which was passed and referred to the railroad committee and the corporation counsel.

A February 8, 1906, storm, coupled with the large number of people wanting to take the trolley cars (and the corresponding increased number of stops) caused every trolley car to run late. By 9:00 p.m., the Colonial City division suspended travel; it did not resume running until the next afternoon. The Kingston City division managed to maintain its normal schedule even with crowded cars. The company tried to clear the Colonial City track on February 9. The superintendent had two trolley cars attached to the snowplow, but when they passed John Street the combined force of the springs on the trolley poles lifted the trolley wire far beyond its normal height, and the absence of a guard wire allowed the charged wire to touch a Hudson River Telephone Company cable. The shorted trolley wire burned in two; one end narrowly missed hitting Mrs. C. B. Stafford and her two children as they crossed the street. For several minutes, there was an intense electrical display. The repairs required many hours.

Problems again hit the Colonial City division on April 9, 1906. Car Number 12 jumped the track at the Clinton Avenue switch, which delayed service thirty minutes until another car came. The same day, two other cars dropped their motor boxes.

In early April 1906, a special committee created by the common council met to investigate whether to allow T-rail in Kingston. T-rail is standard railroad-track rail. Trolley companies running on city streets primarily used girder rail. The shape of this rail prevents the wheels of wagons and carriages and the feet of humans and animals from being caught between the rail and the pavement. Replies from the departments responsible for street surface lines of Manhattan, Brooklyn and Albany were unanimously against the use of T-rails. Further, the secretary of the railroad commission said that he could not recall any system in New York State that was using T-rail. The committee ultimately advised against use of T-rail in Kingston. But Kingston Consolidated, which had been advised to stop installing

T-rail on its track on Broadway near Delaware Avenue in July 1905, submitted another proposal.

The special committee, along with C. Gordon Reel and Chester B. Roe of Kingston Consolidated, went to Amsterdam and Schenectady to inspect T-rail construction in those cities. Eventually, the common council voted ten to eight to allow Kingston Consolidated to lay a temporary stretch of T-rail on the Strand from Abruyn Street to the Ulster & Delaware depot, and on Ferry Street from the ferry house to Broadway.

Kingston Consolidated car #1 jumped the track into Rondout Creek.
Courtesy Al Marquart

Worn equipment and tracks apparently contributed to a spate of accidents over the next few years. On February 19, 1907, at 5:00 p.m., Kingston Consolidated car Number 1 jumped the tracks while on its way to Kingston Point. The car turned toward the Rondout Creek and plunged into the slip of the old Newark Lime & Cement Company. In addition to conductor Walter Flannery and motorman Richard Hauser, there were six passengers on the car: Mrs. John Osterhoudt, wife of the chief engineer of the tug *Washburn*; Sadie

Schutt; Susie McAndrews; John J. Mowell; A. Rossman Haines; and one other unidentified passenger. The car came to rest at a forty-five-degree angle, with its rear wheels resting upon the dock. Local residents, hearing the passengers' screams, quickly rescued them. The passengers helped themselves by crawling on their hands and knees to the rear exit. Mrs. Marchlor, who ran a fruit stand on the Strand, helped Mrs. Osterhoudt, who had a badly cut hand and a broken leg. Several people took Haines, his face covered with blood, to the Mansion House, where Dr. A. A. Stern attended him. It took several stitches to close a long, deep gash above his left eye; he also had a badly lacerated left cheek. Miss McAndrews had a broken rib. Flying glass cut Mowell. Sadie Schutt escaped unhurt. Conductor Flannery was only slightly injured; Hauser, who was thrown from the car before it went into the creek, landed uninjured in the road. The trolley car just grazed the telephone pole on the south side of the slip. Interestingly, the same car had jumped the track at the same spot earlier in the morning. Later in 1907, an inspection was made by the railroad commission. (See Appendix M.)

On April 28, 1908, while on the way up Broadway hill, car Number 19 jumped the track near Mill Street and traveled at least fifty feet over the brick pavement. Opposite Mill Street, the car made a "graceful curve" toward Mill Street and did not stop until nearly over the crosswalk. The car was put back on the track in a short time. The accident, attributed to a worn rail, occurred where the curve began. Since the car had just been repaired and was undergoing testing, there were no passengers aboard.

Late in June, car Number 24 of the Kingston City line went through the crossing gates as a West Shore switch engine was backing down. The trolley motorman reversed the power and backed off the crossing just before the switcher passed; the motorman said the brakes failed. Thirty-eight passengers narrowly escaped serious injury.

In mid-August, car Number 37 on the Colonial City division, in charge of motorman Lemister and conductor Deegan, was coming up Hasbrouck Avenue when it jumped the track on the railroad crossing at Staple's mill. Efforts to get the trolley car back on the track failed. Shortly after the car went off the track, the crew of the car heard the whistle of the 7:45 Ulster & Delaware train. Lemister and Deegan both ran up the track and around the sharp curve to attract the attention of engineer Charles Heldrone, who stopped the train about fifty feet from the derailed trolley. It took about an hour to get the trolley car back on the track.

In late September 1908, the Public Service Commission of the Second District made another inspection as the result of complaints made to the common council about the condition of the Kingston Consolidated Railroad Company's track and cars. During the inspection, Alderman Schermerhorn determined that the road was in poor condition. Assistant Superintendent TeBow admitted the track was in poor condition, but he blamed the city, saying that it would not allow the company to lay new rail. Schermerhorn told inspector Barnes that the common council had disapproved the T-rail the trolley company wanted to use. The common council recommended to the Kingston Consolidated line that it use girder or grooved rail. (See Appendix N.) At the end of December, a Kingston Consolidated representative went to Albany to try to persuade the Public Service Commission to rule in favor of T-rails, a maneuver that didn't work.

On June 2, 1909, Fred T. Ley, of Springfield, Massachusetts, purchased a controlling interest in the Kingston Consolidated Railroad Company. Ley, president of the Board of Trade in Springfield, had twenty years' experience in construction and electric railroads.

In mid-June, Kingston Consolidated asked permission of the common council to put girder rail on Broadway before the city paved it during the summer, which ended the drawn-out battle between the city and the trolley company over what kind of rails could be used in the city. City Engineer Codwise displayed samples of the girder rail, known as Pennsylvania Steel Company's number 243, which weighed ninety pounds per yard.

In late August 1909, Kingston Consolidated asked the Public Service Commission to allow the company to mortgage its property and franchise for $250,000 to the Manhattan Trust Company of New York, and to issue bonds secured by the mortgage for $75,000. The company planned to replace 2.25 miles of track with new girder rail, costing $67,000. The Kingston Consolidated line would use the balance of the proposed mortgage over the following two years for new cars, extensions and improvements to the road.

Shortly before midnight on October 1, a Colonial City trolley car and a coal train collided, killing motorman Fred Roosa. Roosa, making his last run to Ponckhockie, had stopped his car at the junction of the Strand and Ferry Street and then had started down the Strand. At the crossing, the coal train collided with the trolley, crushing the front platform of the trolley car. The force of the impact turned the car toward the Rondout Creek; railroad men had to jack up the coal car to release Roosa's body. Conductor Joseph Hales and yardmaster Joseph VanEtten were on the first car of the Ulster & Delaware train, which was backing up to the coal pockets. Hales said he was blowing the honk hose (a compressed air line with a whistle attached). Coroner Benton planned to hold an inquest.

At the annual stockholder's meeting on January 10, 1909, G. Burton TeBow replaced C. Gordon Reel as superintendent of the trolley line. TeBow had been assistant superintendent.

By April 12, replacement of old track with girder rail had begun, which caused delays and inconvenience to the passengers because of the necessary transfers. A few days later, Kingston Consolidated abandoned the experiment with the T-rail on East Strand because the paving blocks could not be placed properly, and replaced the T-rail with girder rail.

Early in January 1911, the management of the Colonial City division ordered cars halted at Linderman Avenue because contractors on the Washington Avenue sewer line had struck a mud seam between Linderman Avenue and Marius Street, and there were fears that the settling might cause the cars to derail. A wage dispute was settled when Kingston Consolidated announced a one-cent per hour wage increase for conductors and motormen who had been with the company three years or more; the conductors and motormen had asked for a three-cents-per-hour raise. At that time, wages ranged from seventeen-and-a-half to twenty-two cents an hour.

On Friday, February 13, 1914, the worst snowstorm since the Blizzard of '88 hit Kingston. The storm started gently, but by morning there was over a foot of snow on the ground, with drifts to four or five feet. The trolley lines were tied up completely. Kingston Consolidated put the electric snowplow to work early in the storm, but the snow fell so fast that its efforts were obliterated within a half hour. Four cars on the Kingston City division and three on the Colonial division became stalled at various points along the tracks, and to make matters worse the snowplow became stuck. Conductors and motormen joined a gang of shovelers along Broadway.

Two days later, the snowplow still was trying to keep the tracks clear, but snow on the tracks made it difficult to keep the Kingston City division cars running close to schedule. Colonial City cars did not start running until 6:00 p.m. Sunday night, and even then the cars could not run the entire route. By Monday, the cars were running from the corner of Washington Avenue and North Front Street to the powerhouse in Ponckhockie.

By November 1917, it was not enough coal rather than too much snow that was becoming a great concern to the trolley company. The line needed coal to run the power generators for the trolleys' electric power lines. At a meeting of the Chamber of Commerce, directors and Superintendent TeBow decided to apply to the U. S. Fuel Administrator for a power order.

On March 4, 1918 at 6:32 a.m., the New York newspaper train on the West Shore Railroad crashed into a Kingston City car at the Broadway crossing. Wasil Kostocki later died of injuries; Grover Webster sustained a fractured skull and died the next day. Policeman John G. Boyd sustained cuts and internal injuries. He was picked up from the cowcatcher of the engine. Other workers injured included motorman Chester B. Roe, who suffered cuts, a broken thumb and bruises; and conductor William Beadle, who broke his glasses. Passengers injured included Fred W. Sudheimer, Mike Litus, John Grimm, Ben Cohen, J. DeWitt, Daniel Healey, and Denko Melieuzuk. All were treated and released from Kingston City Hospital except Webster, Boyd and Melieuzuk.

At the time of the accident, the trolley car was in charge of conductor Beadle and motorman Roe. Many of the passengers had planned to get off at the West Shore station and board the train that hit the trolley.

The West Short crossing had the reputation of being one of the most dangerous in this section of the state. Witnesses said the crossing gates were up, though gateman Joseph T. Moore claimed he lowered the gates. Coroner E. A. Kelly conducted an inquest.

In mid-March, TeBow offered to lease Kingston Point Park to Kingston City for $1,001. The board of public works referred the matter to the committee on parks. TeBow told the board that receipts for the concessions would be enough to pay the lease. (The terms of the lease are included in Appendix O.) In late April, the board of public works accepted Kingston Consolidated's offer to rent the park for the season, with the option of renewing the lease for an additional five years. The trolley line agreed to furnish the electricity to light the park and to run the merry-go-round.

In early September, in order to reduce the amount of coal needed, the company discussed a "skip-stop" plan--the trolley cars would skip every other stop, resulting in about eight stops per mile; the skip-stop plan was instituted on September 20. (See Appendix P for the stops of the two divisions.) The trolley line reverted to the old system of stops in February 1919. In early September 1918, the employees again asked for a raise, this time to forty cents an hour. (Early in April 1918, Kingston Consolidated granted its conductors and motormen a raise from twenty-seven cents to thirty-one cents an hour. The conductors and motormen had then called off a threatened strike.) TeBow offered thirty-eight cents an hour, but withdrew it after it was rejected. The conductors and motormen hired A. J. Cook to represent the thirty-four car employees, who rejected TeBow's second offer of thirty-eight cents an hour. The dispute was submitted to the War Labor Board.

In November, the railroad company announced that effective December 1, 1918, it would pay the conductors and motormen thirty-eight, thirty-nine or forty cents an hour, depending upon their length of service. In addition, they would receive a retroactive payment for the period September 1 to November 30.

Then, in February 1919, Kingston Consolidated petitioned the Public Service Commission for permission to raise the fare to six cents. Superintendent TeBow submitted financial reports showing that the line was not meeting expenses. Though a six-cent fare would result in a twenty percent increase in fare revenue, experience by other lines such as Poughkeepsie and Newburgh showed that the twenty percent increase usually ended up meaning only a nine to ten percent increase in net earnings because, as fares go up, ridership goes down. In early April, the Public Service Commission authorized the company to raise its fare to six cents starting April 15. The fare was to remain in effect until changed by the Public Service Commission.

Because of accidents at the Broadway crossing, the Public Service Commission ordered the conductors of the Kingston City division to get off the car before crossing the West Shore tracks and to look both ways before getting back on the car. This order went into effect in mid-March 1919.

Late in March, Kingston Consolidated noted that it was the twenty-fifth anniversary of the Colonial City division. Three motormen--Chester B. Roe, Edward H. Butler and Martin Joyce--and three conductors--John J. Fain, Walter Flannery and Frank P. Boyle--had worked for the line during its entire existence. The company also noted that Jefferson Short, of the Kingston City division, had worked for the company since the days of the horse cars.

In mid-April, officer Kuehn painted new "safety zones" on Broadway as an experiment. The safety zones, for the protection of passengers entering or exiting a trolley car, extended nine feet on each side of the trolley track and were about fifty feet by twenty-five feet, extending to the curb. Vehicular traffic could not enter this zone if a pedestrian was inside.

In August, the conductors and motormen of the Kingston Consolidated Railroad Company asked for another raise, this time a twenty-cent increase, to sixty cents an hour. A committee of the conductors and motormen consisting of Frank Boyle, Timothy J. Hannon and Floyd Donahue met with Superintendent TeBow, who told them the trolley line, which was operating at a deficit, could not agree to a pay raise then. Afterwards, the conductors and motormen voted twenty-seven to nine to strike, but at the end of August the men voted not to strike. In February 1920, Kingston Consolidated raised the trolley men's wages from forty to forty-four cents an hour.

UPTOWN—DOWNTOWN; HORSECARS—TROLLEY CARS

Because of accidents occurring at the Broadway crossing, the Public Service Commission and the common council proposed a plan to lower Broadway under the West Shore tracks. In late January 1920, Kingston Consolidated informed the Public Service Commission that it could not pay its $20,000 share toward the Broadway crossing elimination. At the same time, Kingston Consolidated directors voted to abandon the Washington Avenue line between North Front and Marius Streets. Early in February, customers from the affected area held a mass meeting at the courthouse to protest, but on March 1 the stockholders voted to abandon the Washington Avenue line anyway. In mid-March, the company filed a petition to abandon the Washington Avenue track, and by May 1 the City of Kingston filed its opposition.

In early March, Kingston Consolidated announced that it was going to close the Ponckhockie power plant and buy its electric power from the Kingston Gas & Electric Company. (The trolley line eventually closed down the power plant by November 1924, but kept the equipment on standby in case of emergency.)

The Public Service Commission in Kingston held a hearing on May 5 concerning the abandonment of the Washington Avenue line. Before the hearing, Commissioner Hill of the Public Service Commission, Kingston Mayor Canfield, Corporation Counsel William D. Brinnier, Martin S. Decker, and Judge Jenkins (representing citizens opposed to the taking up of the tracks) and G. Burton TeBow made a trip over the tracks in question. The commission heard testimony from Howard Chipp, of the Kingston Consolidated Railroad Company; Brinnier; Canfield; Joseph M. Fowler, of the Chamber of Commerce; Judge Jenkins, John W. Eckert, Daniel B. Deyo, J. DePuy Hasbrouck, M. O. Auchmoody, D. G. Atkins, Henry R. DeWitt, Judge James A. Betts, and Frank W. Brooks for the citizens; and Decker, special counsel for the citizens' committee.

Judge Fowler presented a report prepared by the Chamber of Commerce suggesting that the Public Service Commission make a general survey of the condition of the road. A petition signed by more than fourteen hundred people was presented and made part of the record. Chipp agreed with the recommendation for a general survey.

TeBow presented some of the trolley line's financial data, and Herbert A. Clarke, a consulting engineer, conducted a detailed financial evaluation of the line's assets. According to Clarke's analysis, based on a property valuation of $700,000, the company was earning only 3.9 percent, as opposed to the seven per cent considered normal for a utility. Both Brinnier and Decker immediately objected to the valuation, claiming that the valuation placed on the company when the six-cent fare was granted was $500,000. The commission accepted Clarke's figures, which were broken down by division:

Operating income	basis of	Colonial	Kingston City
Cash fares	Actual	$81,888.71	$102,612.38
Ticket fares	Actual	1,951.84	3,635.48
Chartered car earnings	Actual		15.00
Mail earnings	Actual		696.00
Total revenue from transportation		83,840.55	106,658.86
Advertising and other privileges	Actual	318.18	181.82
Interest revenue	Revenue	70.40	89.59
Misc. rent revenue	Actual	200.00	
Total non-transport revenues		588.58	271.41
Railway operating revenues		84,429.13	106,930.27
Railway operating expenses			
Car miles		92,563.11	55,466.33
Net operating revenue		8,133.98	51,464.04
Taxes accrued on electric railroad			
Capital employed		6,593.03	3,966.11
Gross income		14,692.03	47,435.00
Deduction from gross income			
Interest accrued on funded debt and debenture stocks Cap emp.		21,922.46	12,718.20
Other interest deductions			
Capital employed		192.57	117.10
Amortization of discount on funded debt			
Capital employed		1,119.73	673.31
Misc. debts	Actual	--	--
Total deductions from gross income		22,328.81	13,563.90
Net income		37,021.84	33,932.03

Clarke said the savings generated by abandoning the Washington Avenue track would include wages for four hours each day at forty-four cents an hour, at the current rate of pay ($16.28 a day;

$5,942 a year); on maintenance of equipment ($1,376.05 a year); on repairs ($394.20 a year); and on fuel for power ($9,698.05 a year). The Public Service Commission adjourned the hearing at this point.

To complicate matters, on May 11, 1920, the conductors and motormen requested a pay increase to fifty-five cents an hour, effective May 9. On May 15, Kingston Consolidated decided to withdraw its application for abandonment of the Washington Avenue line. Instead, it joined with the Chamber of Commerce to ask the Public Service Commission to recommend a resolution to the situation. The railroad company withdrew its application for abandonment to the Public Service Commission on March 26. No one objected to the withdrawal. But then, on June 16, the railroad board of directors took the first step to bring before the Public Service Commission, which needed to have proceedings pending before it prior to making the study, the proposed abandonment of portions of the Colonial City division that duplicated the Kingston City division. Kingston Consolidated proposed abandonment of the line on Wall Street and Main Street to Fair Street; on Main Street and Clinton Avenue from Fair to St. James Streets; on Clinton Avenue and Cedar Street from St. James Street to the intersection of Broadway and Thomas Street; on Prince Street and Hasbrouck Avenue between Dederick Street and Delaware Avenue; on Hasbrouck Avenue from Delaware Avenue to East Strand.

On July 20, the stockholders approved the abandonment plans. A few days later, the City of Kingston objected to the application, and Commissioner Hill scheduled a meeting for August 30. Early in August, the common council notified Kingston Consolidated that abandonment of any section would result in the common council rescinding the company's franchise for both divisions. The council's resolution included a proviso requiring bids for busses if the company attempted to take up any track.

Both sides presented their points of view at the hearings before the Public Service Commission on August 30. The hearing continued on September 28, but at this point it appeared that the commission favored a fare increase; early in October, the common council also went on record favoring a fare increase instead of abandonment. By early November, all the parties had agreed to a seven-cent fare, which the Public Service Commission authorized on December 23.

Early in February 1921, Kingston Alderman William B. Martin submitted a resolution allowing both the Colonial and the Kingston City divisions to use the subway to avoid using the Broadway crossing. A month later, Corporation Counsel William D. Brinnier, after discussing the suggestion with TeBow, said that, if implemented, the headway on both divisions would go from ten minutes to fourteen minutes because of increased usage. TeBow also estimated a cost of $2,500 for illuminated signs to show on which division a car was running. While Martin's resolution did not call for illuminated signs, it made sense to have illuminated signs on cars running at night.

In mid-October, Colonial City division cars ran only as far as the switch at the powerhouse on the Strand at the foot of Abruyn Street; jigger service (a one-man car) provided service to Kingston Point until early May, when the Day Line river cruise season opened.

At the end of May 1923, the Kingston Consolidated Railroad Company lost its contract to haul mail between the uptown and downtown substations to the central post office. Peter L. Bonesteel hauled the mail, temporarily, by using trucks.

In late November 1923, Kingston Consolidated applied to the Public Service Commission for permission to raise its fare to ten cents cash or a ticket fare of eight cents because of the increased wages and other expenses. The common council immediately opposed the ten-cent fare. In mid-December, the Public Service Commission held the first hearing on the proposal, and continued hearings in January and February, 1924. Early in February, the common council adopted a resolution against any suspension, elimination or abandonment of service with a fare increase and sent it to the Public Service Commission. In mid-February, Commissioner Parsons of the Public Service Commission concluded that if the citizens of Kingston wanted full service, they would have to pay for it, and despite petitions from the citizens of Kingston, the corporation counsel and the Kingston Taxpayer's Association, in early June the Public Service Commission granted Kingston Consolidated an eight-cent fare.

UPTOWN—DOWNTOWN; HORSECARS—TROLLEY CARS

In mid-December 1924, G. Burton TeBow presented proposed plans for better transportation service in Kingston--using trolley cars and busses. Though not fully developed, TeBow's plan would have replaced duplicate trolley service by busses running in a belt line on both sides of Broadway, a type of system that had proved successful in other cities. Before implementing this proposal and taking it to the Public Service Commission for approval, the trolley company would have to select the routes and obtain a franchise from the common council for a bus line.

In mid-February 1925, the Kingston City Transportation Company submitted a petition to the common council to operate a bus line. The common council referred the petition to the railroad committee and the corporation counsel. The basic plan was to keep the main trolley line (North Front Street to Kingston Point), to discontinue those tracks that paralleled the Kingston City division track, and to replace the abandoned trolley lines and cover new territory with busses. The proposed bus routes were to start at the corner of Washington and Linderman Avenues, and run through Washington Avenue to North Front Street to Clinton Avenue, through Clinton Avenue to Albany Avenue, out Albany Avenue to Flatbush Avenue, through Flatbush Avenue to Downs Street, along Downs Street to Broadway, down Broadway to Cedar Street, through Cedar Street to Clinton Avenue, through Clinton Avenue to Franklin Street, up Franklin Street to Wall Street, through Wall Street to Linderman Avenue, and through Linderman Avenue back to Washington Avenue. Below the West Shore Railroad crossing the bus line would start at the central post office and run through Prince Street to Hasbrouck Avenue, down Hasbrouck Avenue to Delaware Avenue, down Delaware Avenue to Murray Street, through Murray Street to Hasbrouck Avenue; and down Hasbrouck Avenue to the Strand.

On April 23, 1925, the Kingston Consolidated Railroad Company petitioned the Public Service Commission for permission to abandon all of the routes of the former Colonial City Traction Company, except that portion along the Strand to Kingston Point. The company would continue to operate the Kingston City Railroad

Company route. The Public Service Commission granted the company permission to abandon the greater part of the Colonial City division provided the trolley company filed an amended petition within sixty days that did not exclude the subway and included bus service. The Public Service Commission also stipulated that the company institute bus service before the abandonment of the routes.

On September 11, company directors met and approved an amended application to abandon the Colonial City division on or before December 1. Superintendent TeBow said that the abandonment would go forward with or without the busses. When Kingston Consolidated asked to be relieved of having to substitute busses, the Public Service Commission told TeBow, the common council and the Chamber of Commerce to resolve the issue; on September 22, 1925, the common council, at a special meeting, approved the application except for the number of busses required.

Because the company planned to install a loop running through Fair Street to North Front Street, through Wall Street to Main Street, and connecting with the Fair Street track at the corner of Fair and Main Streets, it was necessary to re-lay some track. By September 23, Kingston Consolidated had ordered the new track, even though the common council had not approved the bus franchise and TeBow refused to initiate a new application. Therefore, there was to be no bus service. On October 1, an inquiry found that the Public Service Commission had not made a decision on the application removing the bus requirement as a condition of abandonment.

Early in October, Mayor Block said he had received a proposal from someone in the city to operate a bus line over the route of the Colonial City division, which seemed to confirm rumors of abandonment by mid-November. Block suggested that the common council advertise for additional proposals so that it could select the best proposal. About a week later, the council reported favorably on the application of Howard C. Winne, who proposed to set fares at seven cents, or a book of twenty tickets for a dollar. The common council approved Winne's application the following week.

By November 1, the rails needed to connect the Colonial division with the Kingston City division had arrived. Workers started connecting the two lines at Broadway and Thomas Street. Kingston Consolidated planned to start on connecting at North Front and Wall Streets next, then abandon the Colonial line. On November 11, all trolley traffic was operating over the Kingston City division track except the section from East Strand to Kingston Point.

In mid-November, the common council approved Winne's application to run over the abandoned Colonial City trolley route. But since Winne did not have approval from the Public Service Commission, he could not charge fares (though some passengers made donations). Before Winne could file a petition with the Public Service Commission, the *Freeman* and the *Leader* had to have published the notice of the common council's approval twice. Two days later, Merritt Every offered to run a six-cent bus line and promised to hire all conductors and motormen put out of work by the Kingston Consolidated Railroad Company. The common council rejected Every's application in ten minutes so that it would not interfere with Winne's application.

By the end of November, Kingston Consolidated was dismantling the abandoned Colonial City division. Workers took down all the overhead wires and said they would remove the poles weather permitting.

On December 2, Floyd M. Powell, representing Winne, filed a petition to operate a seven-cent bus line. Citizens of Kingston sent in a petition containing some four thousand signatures approving Winne's plan. In mid-December the Public Service Commission agreed that bus service had to replace the abandoned Colonial division. Commissioner VanVoorhis invited Floyd Powell, Howard Winne, Judge Jenkins, Mayor Block, Judge Irvin, TeBow, and A. C. Connelly (representing the Chamber of Commerce) to the Public Service Commission office in New York City.

At the conference, the commission granted Winne a "certificate of necessity and convenience" to operate a bus line in Kingston. Winne intended to transfer the franchise to the Kingston Consolidated Railroad Company, which planned to operate Yellow Coach busses with a seating capacity of twenty-nine in each bus over Winne's franchise route. A week later, the Public Service Commission granted Winne permission to transfer the certificate to the Kingston City Transportation Company, a subsidiary of Kingston Consolidated. Kingston Consolidated already had ordered the busses; the line was to begin partial operation within two weeks, and over the entire route when all the busses arrived. The bus fare was set at eight cents (five cents for school children on school days from one hour before school until one hour after school). In addition, the company would accept trolley tickets on either the trolley cars or the busses, and passengers could transfer at Cedar Street and Broadway, and at the Rhinecliff ferry. (See Appendix Q.)

The Kingston City Transportation Company planned to begin the new bus service by mid-January 1926. The first loop bus would leave the Strand and Hasbrouck Avenue at 7:00 a.m., the second at 7:07 a.m. After that, a bus would leave the corner every fifteen minutes. A through bus was scheduled to run up Hasbrouck Avenue to Prince Street, to Broadway, to Cedar Street, to Clinton Avenue, to Henry Street, to Wall Street, to Marius Street, to Washington Avenue, to North Front Street, to Clinton Avenue, to Henry Street, to Cedar Street, to Broadway, to Prince Street, and to Hasbrouck Avenue and the Strand. A second through bus route ran through Clinton Avenue to North Front Street, to Washington Avenue, to Marius Street, to Wall Street, to Henry Street, to Clinton Avenue, and so continuing over the same route.

All three busses would meet at the corner of Henry Street and Clinton Avenue; the loop bus would transfer its passengers to the two through busses there. The loop bus ended its run after 9:15 p.m.; the two through busses ran until 11:38 p.m.

Three days after the Public Service Commission's announcement allowing the transfer of Winne's franchise to the Kingston City Transportation Company, Kingston Consolidated Vice President Paige sent Mayor Block a letter requesting transfer of the franchise by the common council before shipment of the busses because of the amount of money involved in purchasing the busses. At this time, Winne was in the process of obtaining temporary busses. Block called a special session of the common council to consider the transfer; two days later the council adopted a resolution transferring Winne's franchise to Kingston City Transportation. During the discussion of the transfer, the common council learned that Kingston Consolidated was paying $15 a day for the temporary busses then on the route, and the company also furnished the drivers, the gas and oil. F. C. Merritt of the Kingston Taxpayer's Association said that the trolley road would telegraph the Yellow Coach Company in Chicago to ship the six busses. The cost of the busses was $54,000.

The Kingston City Transportation Company ordered the busses, which were shipped on February 22 and arrived a couple of weeks later. In the meantime, the temporary, rented busses left the Strand and Hasbrouck Avenue every ten and forty minutes after the hour, arriving at the West Shore on the up trip every twenty-five and fifty-five minutes after the hour; at Henry Street and Clinton Avenue every twenty minutes, and on the even hour. On the return trip, the busses arrived at Henry Street and Clinton Avenue every twenty and fifty minutes after the hour; at the West Shore every twenty-five and fifty-five minutes after the hour; and at the Strand and Hasbrouck Avenue every ten and forty minutes after the hour.

Early in March, the bus company received four of the new busses via the West Shore Railroad, and expected the busses to begin operating by the middle of the month.

Early in May, Kingston Consolidated polled passengers on the trolley line about whether they preferred the trolley to continue using the Colonial subway or to use the Broadway crossing. (The company said that using the Colonial subway required more time than using the Broadway crossing.) Kingston Consolidated, which presumed riders would prefer the Broadway crossing, planned to petition the Public Service Commission to reestablish the Broadway crossing. In fact, results of the passenger poll showed that 998 out of 1456, approximately sixty-nine per cent, favored the Broadway crossing.

When the city bus line started, the belt line busses operated on a half-hour headway. After a month of operation, the bus company tried to increase patronage by running on a twenty-minute headway. After a month's trial, there was no increase in ridership, but the busses traveled farther each day and the drivers had to drive faster to maintain the schedule. Early in November, therefore, the half-hour headway was reinstituted.

Also early in November, Kingston Consolidated and the Kingston City Transportation Corporation filed a petition with the Public Service Commission asking for a fare increase to eight and one-third cents for tickets and a straight ten-cent cash fare on both the bus and trolley lines. The trolley management pointed out that a ten-cent fare had been in effect in Poughkeepsie and Newburgh for some time; Kingston Consolidated cited increased expenses and a general decline in ridership as the reasons for the fare increase. Further, the company claimed that having to use the subway caused interruptions in schedules and increased running time from one end of the two divisions to the other.

The common council opposed the ten-cent fare with only one dissenting vote--from Alderman Molyneaux, a trolley line employee. In mid-November, Kingston Consolidated agreed to withdraw its petition for a fare increase if the common council would withdraw its opposition to the use of the Broadway crossing. Alderman DeGarmo introduced the resolution, which was adopted and referred to the railroad committee. On November 16, 1926, Mayor E. J. Dempsey told the common council that he had heard (unofficially) that Kingston Consolidated had already approached the Public Service Commission for permission to reopen the Broadway crossing, and, in fact, on November 18, the Public Service Commission authorized Kingston Consolidated to operate its cars over the Broadway crossing, provided that the West Short Railroad maintain the metal trolley guard at the crossing in good order, and that a Kingston Consolidated conductor confirmed the tracks were clear in both directions and flagged the trolley car across the tracks. In addition, the commission insisted that the common council withdraw its opposition to using the Broadway crossing. The Public Service Commission ordered the New York Central to restore and maintain the frogs.

At the common council meeting, Alderman DeGarmo, who served on the railroad committee, introduced a resolution withdrawing the opposition of the common council to the use of the Broadway crossing if the trolley withdrew its application for the increased fare. TeBow agreed, provided the common council withdrew its opposition to the use of the Broadway crossing, adding that the trolley line had requested the Public Service Commission to postpone the date of the public hearing for the fare increase until the commission ruled on the Broadway crossing question.

On February 19, 1927, at 11:00 a.m., trolley cars began using the Broadway crossing again, after West Shore employees finished installing the trolley frog. Because of this route change, the trolley could maintain the ten-minute schedule; however, the cars only ran to East Union and North Streets unless a passenger wanted to go to Delaware Avenue and North Street.

In early June 1927, Alderman Haines raised the question of requiring the trolley line to board and discharge passengers from one side of the car only. The common council sent this resolution to the railroad committee, and after a meeting between Alderman DeGarmo and Superintendent TeBow, the company agreed and said that some cars would be ready by August 1.

In mid-June 1928, it was rumored that Kingston Consolidated was planning to ask the common council for permission to replace the trolley cars with busses. Company officials said that new busses would give better service on an even shorter schedule than the present busses. Three days later, the *Freeman* reported that the Kingston City Transportation Corporation would ask the common council on June 19 for authority to operate three bus routes, including the belt line, with a ten-cent cash fare and tokens at nine cents. (See Appendix R for the three proposed routes.) Then, on June 19, the Kingston City Transportation Corporation applied to the common council for authority to discontinue the Kingston Consolidated Railroad Company trolley line and to replace it with bus service. On July 7, the council's railroad committee reviewed the proposed routes. Those attending the meeting included Alderman Leo Care, chair of the committee; Aldermen Fred M. Dressell and John Hull; G. Burton TeBow; County Judge Joseph M. Fowler; George R. Whittaker; and A. Ray Powley of Ponckhockie and E. J. Ritch, citizens who were interested in the Clifton Avenue and Stephan Street belt-line service.

(Powley's concern was the reduction of service to twenty minutes instead of the ten-minute service provided by the trolley company. TeBow reminded Powley that the Washington and Albany Avenue areas were getting thirty-minute service that satisfied its patrons.) One attendee questioned the lack of busses to the Rhinecliff ferry. TeBow replied that the narrowness of the street, parked cars near the ferry, and a taxi stand made it difficult for the busses to get through the street, though he agreed to try to drive a bus through the street to the ferry. The committee agreed to make its report to the common council after the test drive.

On August 7, a delegation of Ponckhockie residents headed by Powley and Eugene B. Carey attended the common council meeting on Kingston City Transportation's application. Powley and Carey emphasized they wanted no changes with the present trolley service; when TeBow was reminded that he wrote a letter three years earlier stating then that the busses could not give as good service as the trolleys, TeBow said that conditions had changed. Finally, on September 19, Kingston City Transportation withdrew its application to replace its trolleys with busses, claiming that various members of the common council had made too many demands.

But by 1929, the finances of the Kingston Consolidated Railroad Company had reached a crisis stage. Near the end of January, the company passed payment on its bonds to conserve cash on hand to meet operating expenses and emergency expenses. By September 9, William D. Brinnier, Jr., on behalf of the Bankers Trust Company, delivered a summons and complaint in an action to foreclose based on the mortgage given to secure payment of bonds issues by Kingston Consolidated when the Kingston City and Colonial City lines merged. Under the terms of the mortgage, if the interest due was unpaid for six months the bank could begin foreclosure, which meant the principal and interest all became due immediately. The collateral for the mortgage included all the busses of the Kingston City Transportation Corporation (since Kingston City Transportation borrowed $18,000 from Kingston Consolidated to acquire the busses when it abandoned the Colonial City line; Kingston City Transportation put up the busses for security for payment of the loan). The bank asked the court to appoint a receiver for both companies, who would sell the assets of the companies at public auction.

Late in September, Brinnier made application for a receiver before New York Supreme Court Judge Pierce H. Russell on behalf of Bankers Trust Company. Judge Russell granted the application and appointed G. Burton TeBow as receiver. TeBow filed a bond for $50,000 and was directed by the court to provide an inventory of all property of both companies, to continue to operate both businesses and to pay all the debts of the companies.

A month later, Brinnier appeared before Judge Russell and requested the court appoint a referee to sell the trolley line, rolling stock and real estate of Kingston Consolidated; on December 6 the court appointed Herbert F. Roy, of Troy, as referee, who set January 21, 1930, at 11:30 a.m. as the date of the auction of the property of the Kingston Consolidated Railroad Company and the Kingston City Transportation Corporation. But on January 21, Roy postponed the sale to March 1, without explanation. On March 1, he postponed the sale again, until March 15.

On March 15, Judge Staley signed an order stopping the foreclosure action. TeBow said that Fred T. Ley, president of the corporation, and his associates had taken over the two companies under agreement between the parties. Further, TeBow said that both the busses and trolley cars would continue to run for the present. The court dissolved the receivership.

On April 1, 1930, Kingston Consolidated again petitioned the common council for permission to replace the trolley cars with busses. As part of the replacement plan, the bus line on Hasbrouck Avenue would also serve the Ponckhockie area, and the company would replace the trolley line with busses operating from North Front and Wall Streets to Fair Street, to Main Street, to Clinton Avenue, to Albany Avenue, to Broadway, to Ferry Street, to Hasbrouck Avenue, to the Strand, to Broadway, and return. The company did not mention bus service on Clinton Avenue.

On April 15, many people from Ponckhockie and from the Clifton Avenue sections of Kingston were at the public hearing called by Mayor Dempsey. The Ponckhockie residents objected to the twenty-minute bus schedule and asked that the company maintain a ten-minute schedule; the Clifton Avenue residents wanted the bus line extended through that section. (See Appendix S for comments made during the public hearing.)

Two weeks later, the bus committee met with officials of Kingston Consolidated to discuss the application for substitute busses. The company was reportedly anxious to get approval so that it could begin operation of the busses during the summer. On May 6, the common council consented to the application. The company agreed to run busses for thirty days over East Chester Street, Clifton Avenue and vicinity to determine whether business conditions justified continuing the route, and it agreed to surrender to the City of Kingston all rights and rights-of-way, grants and franchises for the maintenance of a street railroad, and to pay the city for the use of the streets at the rate of four tenths of one per cent of the gross earnings of the company for each calendar year, with the minimum payment for any one year of $700. The common council gave consent for seventeen years.

Kingston City Transportation established Route 1 between Hasbrouck Avenue and the Strand and Kingston Point, providing enough busses to maintain a twenty-minute schedule; Route 2 would maintain a thirty-minute schedule over the entire route and, in addition to those set forth in the ordinance, would include routes through the following streets: East Chester Street to Highland Avenue, to Clifton Avenue, to Stephan Street, to Foxhall Avenue, to Garden Street, to Prince Street. The modified routes were to be in effect for the first thirty days after the consent, then for the next thirty days the bus company was to follow the routes as outlined in the petition. After the sixty-day period, Kingston City Transportation and the bus committee would develop a route system that would benefit both the bus company and the travelers.

Kingston City Transportation planned to replace the street cars with busses between June 15 and July 1, but it first had to obtain consent of the Public Service Commission. In addition, Kingston City Transportation would have to surrender a consent for the operation of a bus line to Winne and surrender all certificates issued by the Public Service Commission.

On May 6, 1930, Kingston City Transportation applied to the Public Service Commission for permission to operate bus lines under a consent granted by the City of Kingston. Included in the petition were provisions for a ten-cent fare for general transportation and a five-cent fare for school children, and permission to run three bus routes in Kingston. The commission said it would only consider whether it would grant consent for the three bus lines.

William H. Grogan, representing St. Joseph's Church and St. Joseph's Parochial School, raised the only opposition to the petition--he requested the route be changed to avoid congestion and danger to the children near the school. The bus company said it would not change the route. Grogan persisted, claiming that the problem of busses stopping near the church had resulted in the church being used as a waiting room, frequently interfering with church functions and resulting in litter. (Previously, the mayor intervened on the same issue, and the bus company agreed to reroute through Maiden Lane and Crown Street to North Front Street.)

On June 26, the Public Service Commission, at a meeting held in New York City, granted Kingston City Transportation permission to operate the bus lines and to discontinue the operation of the trolley system after the corporation filed a $2,500 personal bond for each vehicle in use, and after it filed a tariff rate with the Public Service Commission. The commission also suggested that St. Joseph's and the common council could resolve the objection to the routing question. Operation of the busses could begin around September 1, the commission suggested, though officials of the bus company said that no date had been fixed for the start of operations. TeBow actually had ordered eight new busses on July 21 (which would give the company a fleet of fourteen), and the company's plan was to begin bus operations September 1.

The eight new busses arrived in Kingston on August 28 and were stored in the car barn. The company also filed a controversial tariff schedule of ten cents with the Public Service Commission.

By this time, the Kingston Consolidated Railroad Company had sold all of its trolley cars and disposed of many closed cars, some of which ended up as summer homes or children's playhouses. Many of the trolley cars were sold to John D. Propheter of Ulster Park, who planned to use them in his amusement park. (See Appendix T for details.)

On August 27, Mayor Dempsey, Corporation Counsel H. H. Flemming, and Alderman Herbert Myers, chair of the bus committee, went to Albany to discuss the proposed ten-cent bus fare, an increase over the eight-cent trolley fare. The next day, Kingston City Transportation filed a supplement to the tariff schedule postponing the effective start date from September 1 to October 1 in order to allow the common council time to discuss the fare matter. The company also announced plans to discontinue the use of tickets and to accept only tokens or cash as fare.

City authorities subsequently requested a change in the proposed Hasbrouck Avenue bus route for the thirty-day trial as follows: Start at North Front and Wall Streets, over North Front Street to Fair Street, to St. James Street, to Clinton Avenue, to Henry Street, to Broadway, to Prince Street, to Clifton Avenue, to Highland Avenue, to East Chester Street, to Hasbrouck Avenue, to Delaware Avenue, to Murray Street, to Hasbrouck Avenue, to the Strand and return. On the Broadway route, the busses would start at North Front and Wall Streets, over North Front Street, to Fair Street, to Main Street, to Clinton Avenue, to Albany Avenue, to Broadway, to Ferry Street, to Hasbrouck Avenue, to the Strand and return. For a period of 30 days, alternate busses would run to Kingston Point unless headway became less than six minutes, in which case every third bus would go to Kingston Point. The company would not implement any route changes until the fare question was resolved.

Joy Roosa, of the board of public works, painted bus stops along the routes. The bus driver was to stop on both corners if passengers were there, otherwise only on the rear corner, until the passengers got acquainted with the new system.

On September 2, the common council discussed the proposed fare increase for the busses. The railroad-and-bus committee recommended that the common council request the Public Service Commission to investigate the necessity of a ten-cent fare. The common council unanimously approved the recommendation. On September 10, the Public Service Commission reviewed the common council's resolution and ruled that since the Kingston City Transportation Corporation was a new company it could set its own rate structure. The Public Service Commission said that after the company had operated for a short time, it could review the rates using actual financial data. Finally, officials of Kingston City Transportation then announced the busses would replace the trolley car service starting October 1, with a fare of ten cents.

On October 1, the Kingston City Transportation Company placed nine busses in service. Route 1 operated on a schedule of less than eight minutes from 7:00 a.m. to 9:00 p.m.; from 6:00 a.m. to 7:00 a.m. and from 9:00 p.m. to midnight the company would maintain a fifteen-minute schedule. Route 2 operated on a thirty-minute schedule. Route 3 operated on a twenty-minute schedule with two busses.

On October 3, officials of Kingston City Transportation requested that passengers use all of their old trolley tickets as soon as possible; the driver would give a token in exchange for a ticket and two cents. The company also asked local companies which had tickets to bring them to the office to redeem them.

The bus company marked the bus stops with orange paint on the street. Automobiles were not supposed to park in these areas. Passengers expressed some confusion about the destination of the busses. Previously, only one route would pass a given stop, but now busses from three different routes could stop at some bus stops.

So, after sixty-five years of the horse car and the trolley car, both have disappeared from the Kingston scene, replaced by busses. Gone is the clang of trolley car bells, but nostalgic memories and fondness for trolleys lingers on. This legacy may be found, relived, and enjoyed by young and old alike in trolley museums scattered across the country. Kingston is fortunate to have one: The Trolley Museum of New York.

Kingston Urban Transportation, 1866-1930: A Pictorial Survey

Ponckhockie-Abruyn Stage Line.
Courtesy Eugene Dauner

Uptown—Downtown; Horsecars—Trolley Cars

Horse car in a parade approaching the Strand on Lower Broadway.
Courtesy Eugene Dauner

Trolley car on Broadway from McEntee Street.
From DeLisser, *Picturesque Ulster*

URBAN TRANSPORTATION IN KINGSTON, NEW YORK, 1866-1930

Horsecar in a Broadway parade, 1880s.
Courtesy The Trolley Museum of New York

UPTOWN—DOWNTOWN; HORSECARS—TROLLEY CARS

Trolley car on Broadway from Ferry Street
From DeLisser, *Picturesque Ulster*

Colonial City trolley car on Hasbrouck Ave., from Delaware Ave.
From DeLisser, *Picturesque Ulster*

URBAN TRANSPORTATION IN KINGSTON, NEW YORK, 1866-1930

Above: Trolley car on Broadway
Courtesy Joseph Fautz

Below: Kingston Point Park station
Courtesy The Trolley Museum of New York

Uptown—Downtown; Horsecars—Trolley Cars

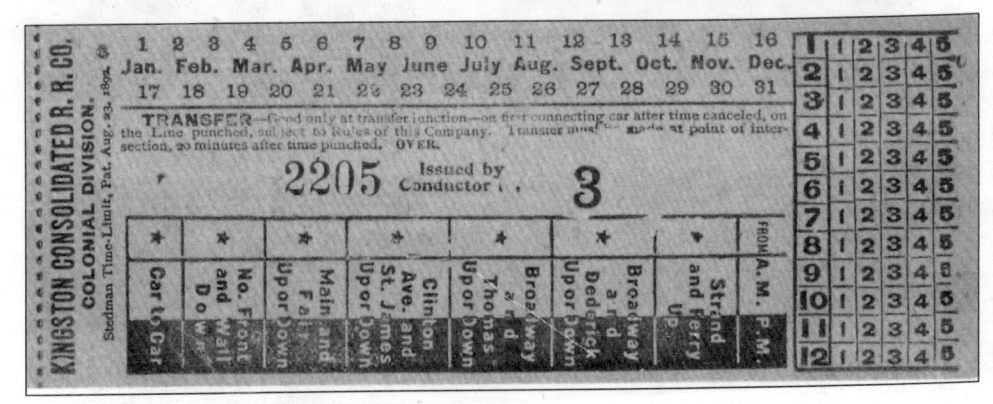

Trolley cars # 38 & 46 at the intersection of Ferry St. and the Strand.
Courtesy The Trolley Museum of New York

Kingston Consolidated ticket and a transfer.
Courtesy The Trolley Museum of New York

Above: Trolley car on Broadway showing post office and Y.M.C.A.
Courtesy The Trolley Museum of New York

Right: Trolley car on Broadway, westvfrom American Cigar Factory
Courtesy The Trolley Museum of New York

Below: Trolley car on Lower Broadway, Rondout.
Courtesy Eric A. Fedde

UPTOWN—DOWNTOWN; HORSECARS—TROLLEY CARS

Above: Trolley car on North Front Street.
Below: Trolley car on Wall Street, looking south.
Courtesy The Trolley Museum of New York

Above: Colonial City car # 6 and sprinkler car.
Below: Repairing track, Broadway in front of old post office, ca 1909.
Courtesy The Trolley Museum of New York

UPTOWN—DOWNTOWN; HORSECARS—TROLLEY CARS

Above: Running to catch a trolley car on Broadway hill.
Courtesy The Friends of Kingston
Below: Kingston City trolley car # 46
Courtesy The Trolley Museum of New York

Appendix A - Directors of the Kingston Horse Railroad Company

1864
Robert H. Atwater
Elihu J. Baldwin
Thomas Cornell
Jansen Hasbrouck
Jonathon H. Hasbrouck
Lewis N. Hermance
Michael J. Madden
William C. More
Henry A. Samson
Henry D. H. Snyder
Lorenzo A. Sykes
Elias T. Van Nostrand
William H. Wells

1868
Robert H. Atwater
Thomas Cornell
Samuel D. Coykendall
S. G. Dimmick
Jansen Hasbrouck
Lewis D. Hornbeck
J. G. Lindsley
William Lounsberry
Michael J. Madden
Henry A. Samson
H. Schoonmaker
Lorenzo A. Sykes
Elias T. Van Nostrand

1871
Anthony Benson
Charles Bray
Thomas Cornell
Samuel D. Coykendall
Patrick J. Flynn
William M. Hayes
Lewis N. Hermance
John Hussey
James G. Lindsley
William Lounsberry
Jacob Rider
Hiram Schoonmaker
Elias T. Van Nostrand

1872
Anthony Benson
Charles Bray
Thomas Cornell
Samuel D. Coykendall
Patrick J. Flynn
William M. Hayes
Lewis N. Hermance
John Hussey
James G. Lindsley
William Lounsberry
Jacob Rider
Hiram Schoonmaker
Elias T. Van Nostrand

1873
Anthony Benson
Charles Bray
Thomas Cornell
Samuel D. Coykendall
Patrick J. Flynn
William M. Hayes
John Hussey
James G. Lindsley
William Lounsberry
Jacob Rider
Artemas Sahler
Hiram Schoonmaker
Elias T. Van Nostrand

August 1874
Reuben Bernard
Samuel C. Dimmick
Patrick J. Flynn
Manasseh Longyear
William Lounsberry
Artemas Sahler
Elias T. Van Nostrand
Benjamin J. Winne
Cornelius C. Winne
Davis Winne
Henry W. Winne
William Winne

1875
Reuben Bernard
Samuel C. Dimmick
Patrick J. Flynn
Manasseh Longyear
Edward O'Reilly
Edward Sherer
Elias T. Van Nostrand
J. Webber
Benjamin J. Winne
Cornelius C. Winne
Davis Winne
Henry W. Winne
William Winne

1876
Reuben Bernard
John W. Cole
Elijah DuBois
Samuel C. Dimmick
Patrick J. Flynn
Manasseh Longyear
Edward O'Reilly
Elias T. Van Nostrand
Benjamin J. Winne
Cornelius C. Winne
Davis Winne
Henry W. Winne
William Winne

1877
Reuben Bernard
John W. Cole
Elijah DuBois
Samuel C. Dimmick
Patrick J. Flynn
Manasseh Longyear
Edward O'Reilly
Elias T. Van Nostrand
Benjamin J. Winne
Cornelius C. Winne
Davis Winne
Henry W. Winne
William Winne

Appendix B - Kingston City Railroad Time Table

Lv Kingston 6:00 a.m. and every 20 minutes thereafter, until 10 o'clock a.m.
    Then every 10 minutes until 8 o'clock p.m.
Lv Rondout 6:40 a.m. and every 20 minutes thereafter, until 10 o'clock a.m.
    Then every 10 minutes until 8 o'clock p.m.
After 8 p.m. the cars will leave both ends of the route at 8:30; 9:00; 9:30; 10:00 p.m.
A car will await the arrival of steamers Thomas Cornell and James W. Baldwin.

TICKETS can be obtained at Forsyth & Wilson and E. Winters uptown and W. Winter and the office of Company downtown and of the Superintendent at the following rates:
    12 through tickets $1.00
    10 school tickets   50
    11 way tickets   50

[Source: Kingston *Daily Freeman*, January 4, 1881.]

Appendix C - Kingston City Railroad Financial Reports

Sep. 8, 1892. THE KINGSTON CITY RAILROAD Its report for the Year Which Ended June 30, 1892
Albany Sep 8 - The Kingston City Railroad Company has just filed its annual report with the railroad commissioners for the year ending June 30. Its income account shows:

Gross earnings from operations	$ 31,806.01
Less operating expenses	22,767.71
Net earnings from operation	9,038.30
Deductions from income as follows:	
Taxes on property	571.26
Taxes on earnings and capital	274.98
Taxes other than above	29.66
Interest on funded debt, due and accrued	1,910.00
Net income from all sources	6,252.40
Payments from net income as follows, viz:	
Dividends declared 10 per cent on capital stk	5,000.00
Surplus for year ending June 30, 1892	1,252.40
Surplus up to June 30, 1891	11,051.81
Total surplus June 30, 1892	12,304.21

The amounts expended by the company during the year for betterment was $240, all of which amount was spent in additional equipment.

The total operating expenses, $22,767, included the following among other expenditures: Salaries of general officers and clerks, $1,770; wages of conductors and drivers, $4,971; wages of watchmen, starters, switchmen, etc., $4,817; renewals of horses and mules, $1,185; light and fuel, $350

The company reports that the total length of its road (single track) is 2.77 miles. Its equipment comprises 8 box cars, not motors; no open cars, no motors; 42 horses and mules.

During the year the number of passengers carried was 489,320. The average number of the company's employees (including officials) during the year was 23.

There was one accident caused during the twelve months by the road's operation which proved fatal.

GENERAL BALANCE SHEET

Assets		Liabilities	
Cost of road	$ 79,855.11	Capital stock	$ 50,000.00
Cost of equipment	9,556.81	Funded debt	31,000.00
Cash on hand	8,284.13	Open accounts	2,058.16
Open accounts	600.32	Profit and loss, surplus	15,304.21
Supplies on hand	66.00	Total	98,362.37
Total	$98,362.37		

[Source: Kingston *Daily Freeman*, September 8, 1892.]

May 14, 1894.   The Kingston City Railroad Company has just filed the following report with the railroad commissioners for the quarter ended March 31st last.

	1894	1892
Gross earnings	$10,709	$ 6,892
Operating expenses	6,991	5,323
Net earnings	$3,718	$ 1,569

The general balance sheet shows as follows:

Assets	
Cost of road & equipment	$308,487
Supplies on hand	240
Cash on hand	4,181
Total	$312,908

Fixed Charges		
Interest on funded debt	$2,040	477
Taxes on property	211	143
Taxes on earnings etc.	77	69
Taxes other	6	6
Net income	$1,390	$874

Liabilities	
Capital stock	$150,000
Funded debt	155,000
Interest on funded debt, due and accrued	950
Due for wages and supplies	966
Profit and loss, surplus	5,992
Total	$312,908

[Source: Kingston *Daily Freeman*, May 14, 1894.Sep. 3, 1894.]

Albany Sep 3 - The Kingston City Railroad Company has just filed its annual report with the railroad commissioners for the year ending June 30. Its income account shows:

Gross earnings from operations	$ 46,467
Less operating expenses	29,038

Urban Transportation in Kingston, New York, 1866-1930

Net earnings from operation 17,429
Deductions from income as follows:
Taxes on property 879
Taxes on earnings and capital. 233
Taxes other than above. 22
Interest on funded debt, due and accrued. 8,264
Net income from all sources 8,031
Payments from net income as follows, viz:
Dividends declared 2.5 per cent on capital stock . . 3,750
Surplus for year ending June 30, 1894 4,281
Surplus up to June 30, 1893 16,924
Less Depreciation. 18,924
Total surplus June 30, 1892 . . . . ,281

The amounts expended by the company during the year for betterment was $214,504, of which amount $218,561 was spent on the road, and $4,056 was received in sale of rolling stock. The principal items of expenditures under the head of betterments were the following: Road built by contract $225,000; real estate $9,975.

The total operating expenses, $29,038, included the following among other expenditures: Salaries of general officers and clerks, $1,574; wages of conductors and motormen, $8,770; wages of watchmen, starters, switchmen, etc., $3,331; wages of engineers, firemen, and other power house employees, $3,810.

The company reports that the total length of its road (single track) is 2.8 miles. Its equipment comprises 6 motor cars.

During the year the number of passengers carried was 929,348. The average number of the company's employees (including officials) during the year was 27. There were no accidents during the twelve months caused by the road's operation.

[Source: Kingston *Daily Freeman*, September 3, 1894. Jan. 25, 1895.]

THE KINGSTON CITY RAILROAD'S STATEMENT TO RAILROAD COMMISSIONERS

Albany Jan 24 - The report of the Kingston City Railroad Company for the quarter ending November 31st last, as filed with the railroad commissioners shows as follows:

GENERAL BALANCE SHEET

	1894	1893
Gross earnings	$ 13,382	$12,093
Operating expenses	7,648	8,092
Net earnings	5,734	4,001
Gross income from other sources	none	none
Gross income	5,734	4,001
Deductions from income as follows:		
Taxes on property.	220	250
Taxes on earnings and capital stock.	58	71
Taxes other than above	4	6
Interest on funded debt, due and accrued	2,040	none
Dividends...	4,500	none
Deficit	1,087	1,634 surplus

Assets
Cost of road $312,852
Supplies on hand. 899
Due by companies and individuals. 37
Cash on hand 3,129
Total $316,917

Liabilities
Capital stock $150,000
Funded debt 156,000
Interest on funded debt, due and accrued 2,125
Due for wages and supplies. 1,182
Profit and loss, surplus 7,610
Total 316,917

[Source: Kingston *Daily Freeman*, January 25, 1895. Aug. 16, 1895.]

The following is a comparative statement of the earnings and expenses of the Kingston City Railroad Company for the year ending June 30, 1894 & 1895.

	1894	1895
Gross earnings	$46,467.41	$50,229.65
Operating expenses	29,037.50	31,403.83
	$17,429.91	$18,825.82

Other disbursements	1894	1895
Int. on funded debt	$8,264.17	$8,160.00
Taxes	1,134.06	1,416.45
Dividend	3,750.00	9,000.00
	$13,148.23	$18,576.45
Surplus for the year	$4,281.68	$249.37

[Source: Kingston *Daily Freeman*, August 16, 1895.]

Appendix D - Agreements, Contracts and Letters

Agreement between Ulster and Delaware Railroad and the Colonial City for the repair of the Ulster and Delaware tunnel

WHEREAS The Colonial City Electric Railway Company, its agents, servants and contractors in the construction of its Road, and in or about the month of December 1893, injured, impaired and weakened the Tunnel or Arch of the Ulster & Delaware Railroad Company at Hasbrouck Avenue and Delaware Avenue, in the City of Kingston, Ulster County, N. Y.-

NOW THEREFORE, This agreement made the 5th day of April , 1894 between the said Ulster & Delaware Railroad Company of the first part and the Colonial City Electric Railway Company of the second part,-

WITNESSETH, The party of the first part for and in consideration of the covenants to be kept and performed, and the moneys to be paid by the party of the second part as hereinafter set forth, hereby agree to fully restore said Tunnel or Arch, and repaid all injuries and damages thereto occasioned by the party of the second part, but without needless or unnecessary expenses. All such work and repairs to be made under the direction and supervision of the Engineer of the party of the first part, and to be fully completed within six months from the date hereof.

And the party of the second part for the consideration above and for the further sum of ONE DOLLAR to it paid by the party of the first part for itself, its successors and assigns, covenants to and with the party of the first part, its successors and assigns to pay to the party of the first part the full amount already paid or to be paid laid out and expended by the party of the first part in and upon such repairs, and restoration of such Tunnel or Arch, made or to be made as aforesaid by the party of the first part including all work and labor thereon; superintendence thereof, sand the material therefor furnished by the party of the first part, or heretofore by it furnished, such payment to be made by the party of the second part in cash within three days after the receiving of an account from the party of the first part, of all the costs and expenses of such repairs.

IT IS STIPULATED AND AGREED, That such account and expenses of repairs may be served on the party of the second part by delivering the same to the President thereof, or to Alva S. Newcomb, at his office in the city of Kingston, Ulster Co, N. Y.

Nothing herein contained shall be construed to release the party of the second part from any liability from damage to the track or rolling stock, or other property of the party of the first part, caused by the falling of said Tunnel or Arch or any portion thereof, while the same remains in its present condition and unrepaired state.

IT IS FURTHER STIPULATED AND AGREED, By and between the parties of this instrument, that the said party of the second part shall upon the execution of this Contract, make execute and deliver to the party of the first part a Bond for the performance of the covenants, conditions and agreements mentioned and contained in this Instrument, on the part of the party of the second part in the penalty of $5,000 with sufficient sureties.

AND this Contract at the option of the party of the first part be void and of no effect until said Bond shall be so executed and delivered and shall be approved in writing as to form and sufficiency of sureties by the President of the party of the first part.

IN WITNESS WHEREOF, the said parties have hereunto caused their respective corporate seals duly attested by their proper officers, to be set the day and year first above mentioned.

Signed, Sealed and Delivered
in the Presence of

COLONIAL CITY ELECTRIC RY. CO.
by Wendell Goodwin
Vice-President
The Ulster & Delaware R.R.
by H. G. Young
President

[Source: Collection of Eugene Dauner]

URBAN TRANSPORTATION IN KINGSTON, NEW YORK, 1866-1930

REED & McKIBBIN,
ELECTRIC STREET RAILWAY CONTRACTORS,
80 BROADWAY, NEAR WALL ST.,
NEW YORK.

New York, April 27, 1894.

H. C. Soop, Genl. Mgr.,
    Ulster & Delaware R.R., Co.,
        Rondout, N.Y.

Dear Sir:

    We understand that the damages to the tunnel on your road, in the City of Kingston, caused in some way by the construction of the Colonial City Railway, have been repaired to your satisfaction, and under your immediate supervision and direction.

                  Yours very truly,

                  Reed & McKibbin

[Source: Collection of Eugene Dauner]

Agreement Between West Shore Railroad and Colonial City Electric Company Trestle Agreement

THIS AGREEMENT, made and entered into on this 18th day of July 1894, by and between the WEST SHORE RAILROAD COMPANY and the NEW YORK CENTRAL AND HUDSON RIVER RAILROAD COMPANY, as Lessee of the West Shore Railroad, parties of the first part, and the COLONIAL CITY ELECTRIC RAILWAY COMPANY, party of the second part, WITNESSTH, that

    Whereas the West Shore Railroad Company is the owner of a certain line of steam railroad extending through the City of Kingston, County of Ulster and State of New York, and across Smith Street in said city, of which railroad the New York Central and Hudson River Railroad Company is lessee; and the said party of the second part is a street surface railway corporation engaged in the construction of a line of electric surface railway in said City of Kingston, upon and along a route extending through said Smith Street from Grand Street to Cornell Street; and

    Whereas certain proceedings instituted by the party of the second part for the purpose of acquiring a crossing over the tracks of the West Shore Railroad on said Smith Street are now pending and a certain action instituted by the parties of the first part against the party of the second part is now pending, and

    Whereas the parties hereto have by agreement arranged for the crossing of said tracks of the parties of the first part by the party of the second part in a manner satisfactory to all said parties, as is hereinafter set forth and provided;

    NOW, THEREFORE, for and in consideration of the premises and of the sum of One Dollar by the party of the second part to the parties of the first in hand paid, the receipt whereof is hereby acknowledged, and in further consideration of the several covenants and agreements hereinafter contained the parties hereto do jointly and severally mutually agree as follows:--

    FIRST: The proceedings instituted by the party of the second part for the acquiring of a crossing over the tracks of the West Shore Railroad and the injunction action aforesaid shall be discontinued and abandoned without costs or damages to either party as against the other; the party of the second part to pay the fees of the Commissioner in the proceedings instituted by it.

SECOND: The parties of the first part hereby give and grant unto the party of the second part the right to cross their aforesaid railroad and the right of way and tracks thereof solely upon an elevated structure to be built by said party of the second part upon and along said Smith Street, and having two spans with the necessary support at the junction of the two spans at a point within said right of way; PROVIDED, HOWEVER, that the said structure shall cross the said right of way and tracks at a height of not less than twenty-one (21) feet in the clear between the lowest part of the said structure and the top of the rails of the aforesaid railroad of the parties of the first part. And PROVIDED, FURTHER, that the party of the second part shall at any time hereafter upon six months written notice and request given to it by the parties of the first part, remove the said support to such other position upon the right of way of the parties of the first part as may be designated by them, or remove the same off said right of way.

THIRD: The party of the second part hereby agrees that it will erect the said elevated structure in a good and substantial manner, according to plans approved by the parties of the first part, and will at all times maintain the same at its own sole costs, charge and expense in a safe and sound condition and will at all times hold and save harmless the parties of the first part from any liability, loss or damage which may accrue to the parties of the first part or to either of them or their employees or their property, or the lives or persons or property of other persons lawfully using the railroad of the said parties of the first part, arising out of or from the erecting and maintenance of the overhead crossing and support hereinbefore provided for or out of or from operation of the railroad of the party of the second part thereon.

IN WITNESS WHEREOF the several parties hereto have caused this instrument to be signed by the respective executive officers, thereunto duly authorized; and sealed with their respective corporate seals duly attested, all on the day and year first above written.

                        The New York Central & Hudson River Railroad
                        by C. C. Clark, vice-president
                        West Shore Railroad Company
                        by Ashbal Green, vice-president
                        Colonial City Electric Railway Co.
                        by Wendell Goodwin, vice-president

[Source: Collection of Eugene Dauner]

WENDELL GOODWIN,
FREDERICK SWIFT,
66 BROADWAY,

NEW YORK, July 16, 1894.

H. C. Soop, Esq.,

       Kingston, N. Y.

Dear Sir,

       Enclosed herewith I beg to hand you copy of the agreement which we today had prepared by our counsel, Messrs. Davies, Stone & Auerbach in the matter of the West Shore crossing. I took the same to their office in New York today to have it looked over, and I hope, signed. Meanwhile, will you do me the favor to have a form similar, prepared for the Ulster & Delaware crossing, eliminating such portions of the enclosed as bear on the litigation which is referred to, which does not exist in the case of the Ulster & Delaware Road, but retaining all that has direct reference to the situation.

I believe you have a blueprint for the supports or bents that we desire to locate on your right of way, and would ask that you kindly consider same a part of the agreement, which is to be prepared by you. Should you desire other forms of plans, I shall be pleased to submit them at once.

I hope to see Mr. Young here tomorrow, when I will discuss a copy of the enclosed with him, and also the situation of the abutting property of the Cornell Estate.

Thanking you for your promptness in these matters,

I am,

Yours very truly,

Wendell Goodwin

Enclosure.

[Source: Collection of Eugene Dauner]

Letter from Wendell Goodwin to H. C. Soop

Wendell Goodwin
Frederick Swift
66 Broadway

NEW YORK, July 18, 1894

H. C. Soop, Esq.,
    Rondout, N. Y.

Dear Sir,
    I beg to acknowledge the receipt of your telegram of this date, as follows:- "Will draft agreement for Ulster & Delaware and submit to President as soon as possible after receiving copy of West Shore Agreement". You will, I trust, receive this copy of the West Shore Agreement referred to in my letter of this morning at the same time you get this, and I thank you for your promise to attend to it promptly.

Yours very truly,
(signed) Wendell Goodwin

Uptown—Downtown; Horsecars—Trolley Cars

A note was written on the letter by Soop: When last I saw you I believe you were to bring it down for signature yourself to the accompaniment of ... Is this not so? [Letter from Goodwin to Soop dated July 18, 1894]

WENDELL GOODWIN,
FREDERICK SWIFT,
66 BROADWAY.

NEW YORK, July 18, 1894.

H. C. Soop, Esq.,
    Rondout, N. Y.

Dear Sir,

    I confirm my telegram to you, of today, and beg to advise having seen Mr. Young, and shown him the copy of the Agreement forwarded you, and also blueprints of the situation as regards the Ulster & Delaware Railroad, and the abutting Cornell properties.

    He said he expected to hear from you today in reference to same.

    In accordance with the contents of the telegram I beg to enclose herewith, copy of the Agreement which after examination has been approved in this form by the West Shore Railroad, and has passed their Board.

    Mr. Young spoke to me about a clause covering removal of the structure by the party of the second part, in case they abandoned the overhead crossing. You can add this if you choose, to your Agreement.

    I spoke of this matter to Judge Greene, and he said he did not care to incorporate it as in case we abandoned it, they would burn it down.

URBAN TRANSPORTATION IN KINGSTON, NEW YORK, 1866-1930

WENDELL GOODWIN,
FREDERICK SWIFT,
66 BROADWAY,

NEW YORK,

Soop-2.

    I regret that in the copies of the Agreement furnished you and the West Shore Railroad, the title of Colonial City Electric Railway Company was incorrectly written as Colonial Railway Company and this was really the main change in the wording suggested by Judge Green as you will see.

    I beg also to advise that a Meeting of the Board of Directors of Colonial City Electric Railway Company was held yesterday in accordance with instructions from me, and I have duly attested copy of the Minutes authorizing me to sign the said Agreement as Vice President, and affix the seal.

    Therefore, when you have received same from Mr. Young will you kindly forward to this office for signature.

        Yours very truly,

        Wendell Goodwin

Enclosures.

[Source: Collection of Eugene Dauner]

Draft copy of agreement between Ulster & Delaware and Colonial City

This agreement allowed Colonial City to cross U & D tracks on elevated structure

THIS AGREEMENT. Made and entered into on this   day of July 1894, by and between THE ULSTER & DELAWARE RAILROAD COMPANY, party of the first part, and, THE COLONIAL CITY ELECTRIC COMPANY, party of the second part, WITNESSETH:

    WHEREAS, The Ulster & Delaware Railroad Company is the owner of a certain line of steam Railroad extending through the City of Kingston, County of Ulster, and State of New York, and crossing Cornell street in said City; and the said party of the second part is a street surface railway corporation engaged in the construction of a line of electric surface railway, in said City of Kingston, and upon and along a route extending through Cornell street, from Broadway to Tremper Avenue:

NOW THEREFORE, for and in consideration of the premises, and the sum of One Dollar by the party of the second part to the party of the first part in hand paid, the receipt whereof is hereby acknowledged, and the further consideration of the several covenants and agreements hereinafter contained, the parties hereto do jointly and severally mutually agree as follows:
1st; The party of the first part hereby gives and grants unto the party of the second part, the right to cross their aforesaid Railroad, and the right-of-way and tracks thereof, solely and only upon an elevated structure to be built by said part of the second part, upon and along said Cornell street, and having two spans with the necessary support at the junction of the two spans sat a point within said right-of-way; providing however that the said structure shall cross the said right-of-way and tracks at a height of not less than twenty-one feet between the lowest part of said structure and the top of the rails of the aforesaid Railroad of the party of the first part.

And provided further, that the party of the second part shall at any time hereafter upon six months notice and request given to it by the party of the first part, remove the said support to such other position upon the right-of-way of the party of the first part as may be designated by them, or remove the same off said right-of-way.

It being understood and agreed, that all rights and privileges by the terms hereof or giving by the party of the first part to the party of the second part, shall be absolutely concluded and determined by said six months notice in writing.

2nd: The party of the second part hereby agree that it will erect the said structure in a good and substantial manner, according to the plans approved by the party of the first part, and will at all maintain at its sole cost, charge and expense in a safe and sound condition; and will at all times hold, and save harmless the party of the first part, from any liability loss or damage which may accrue to the party of the first part or to either of them, or to their employees, or their property, or the lives of persons, or property of other persons, lawfully using the Railroad of the said party of the first part, arising out of or from the erecting and maintenance of the overhead crossing hereinbefore provided, or out of or from the operation of the Railway of the party of the second part thereon.

IN WITNESS WHEREOF, the several parties hereto have caused this Instrument to be signed by their respective Executive Officers, thereunto duly authorized, and sealed with their respective corporate seal, duly attested, on the day and year first written above.
[Source: Collection of Eugene Dauner]

Agreement Between the Ulster & Delaware and Colonial City for the Colonial to cross the U & D tracks at grade

THIS AGREEMENT, Made the   day of September, 1894, BETWEEN THE ULSTER & DELAWARE RAILROAD COMPANY, of the first part and the COLONIAL CITY ELECTRIC RAILWAY COMPANY of the city of Kingston, N. Y. and John E. Kraft of the city of Kingston and Arthur W. Walradt of the city of New York as receivers of the property of said Colonial City Electric Railway Co., parties of the second part, WITNESSETH;-

Whereas, the Ulster & Delaware Railroad Co., is the owner of certain line of Steam Railroad, extending through the city of Kingston, Ulster County, and State of New York, and crossing Cornell Street in said city; and the said parties of the second part are the Receivers of the property of the Colonial City Electric Railway Company, a street surface Railway Corporation engaged in the construction of a line of surface railway in said city of Kingston, upon and along a route extending through Cornell street from Broadway to Tremper Avenue.

Now therefore, the party of the first part for and in consideration of the covenants to be kept and performed and the moneys to be paid by the parties of the second part as hereinafter set forth, hereby grants to the parties of the second part and their successors and assigns the right to cross at grade, until the 1st day of June 11895 and no longer, the present and any future tracks of the party of the first part at Cornell Street; and the said parties of the second part for the consideration above and the further sum of ONE DOLLAR paid them by the party of the first part, for themselves, their successors and assigns covenant to and with the party of the first part its successors and assigns as follows:-

The said crossing of the said tracks of the said party of the first part shall be made by the parties of the second part in a manner satisfactory to the Engineer of the party of the first part; and the parties of the second part shall at all times and at their own proper costs keep and maintain the crossings made by them in good repair and condition, and generally bear and pay all expenses and cost present and future in laying down constructing, maintaining and renewing the crossings of the track of the party of the first part now in place or any other tracks that the party of the first part may hereinafter lay at said Cornell Street, including labor and material.
SECOND
That any elevated wires used by the parties of the second part shall be elevated at least twenty-one feet above the top of rails of the party of the first part.
THIRD
The party of the first part may if they deem it necessary and at their option at any time after the construction and operation of the said Colonial City Electric Railway upon and over said crossing, keep and provide a watchman or watchmen at such crossing; that such watchman or watchmen shall be selected by the party of the first part and shall be paid for their services by the parties of the second part, and in the event of the erection by the party of the first part of safety gates at said crossing, the watchman referred to above shall operate the gates, and in case of refusal or neglect by the parties of the second part to pay, as herein provided, a right of action to recover said money paid for the cost of such services by the party of the first part, shall accrue to the party of the first part against the parties of the second part.
FOURTH
That the said parties of the second part shall pay the party of the first part for all damages to their track, rolling stock and other property which shall be caused by accident resulting from the carelessness neglect or inattention of any of the employees of the parties of the second part.
FIFTH
That until it shall be deemed advisable by the party of the first part to establish a permanent watchman at such crossing the parties of the second part shall cause the cars of the Colonial City Electric Railway Co., to come to a full stop at a distance of not more than fifty feet from the nearest rail of the track of the party of the first part; and not proceed to cross the said track until notified to do so by an employee of one of the parties hereto authorized to give such notice.
SIXTH
Provided further that the parties of the second part shall on or before the 1st day of June 1895 remove from the right-of-way of the party of the first part, the ties, rails, earth, stone, and all materials by them placed on same and used for the purposes of such crossing, and shall in every way and particular restore said crossing to the same condition , the same was in before used by the parties of the second part and shall quit and abandon the crossing of the tracks of the party of the first part at Cornell Street; and in the event that the party of the second part shall fail or neglect to so remove such ties, rails and materials from said right-of-way on or before the first day of June 1895 as herein provided than and in such case the party of the first part may remove the same. That all rights and privileges by the terms hereof, given by the party of the first part to the parties of the second part, shall be absolutely concluded, ended and determined on the 1st day of June, 1895.
SEVENTH
Provided further that the parties of the second part shall carry said Colonial City Electric Railway over the West Shore Railway at Smith Avenue on a bridge and trestle in the manner and at the place required by the New York Central and Hudson River Railroad Company.
EIGHT
Nothing herein contained shall be construed to give, grant or convey any further or other rights than the right to the parties of the second part to cross the track of the party of the first part at Cornell Street as hereinbefore expressed temporarily and to the 1st day of June 1895.
NINTH
Nothing herein contained shall in any way affect, change or modify any of the agreements made in writing between the party of the first part and the Colonial City Electric Railway Company

now existing respecting the crossing of the tracks of the party of the first part in the city of Kingston.

TENTH

That the right and authority of the parties of the second part as receivers, as aforesaid, to make and execute this agreement shall be conferred by order of the Supreme Court of the State of New York, duly entered in the office of the clerk of Ulster County, before this agreement shall become operative and valid.

IN WITNESS WHEREOF, the said John E. Kraft and Arthur E. Walradt, as Receivers of said Colonial City Electric Railway Company, have subscribed their names and affixed their seals as said receivers to these presents, and said Colonial City Electric Railway Company and said Ulster & Delaware Railroad Company have caused their respective seals to be affixed and these presents to be subscribed by their respective Presidents on the day and year first above written.

[Source: Collection of Eugene Dauner]

```
                    WEST  SHORE  RAILROAD
                    N.Y.C.& H.R R.R.Co., Lessee,
                       No.5 Vanderbilt Avenue.
J.D.Layng, General Manager.

Mr.H.G.Young,

          President, Ulster and Delaware R.R., Rondout, N.Y.

Dear Sir:--

             Absence from home has prevented an earlier reply to

yours of September 21st in answer to mine of the 15th in relation to

the crossings at grade proposed by the Colonial City Ry in Kingston

             The action of your General Counsel in agreeing to

this was no doubt influenced by local pressure which has been

exerted upon the officers of this Company in every imanigable way

and which we have steadfastly refused to acknowledge.  We will

not consent to the temporary grade crossing over the West Shore

and I do trust you will not allow the contract for the Ulster and

Delaware to be executed until they have succeeded in getting over

the West Shore Railroad by contract or otherwise.

                     Very truly yours,

                    ( Signed )    J.D.Layng,

                                    General Manager.
```

[Source: Collection of Eugene Dauner]

The Kingston Leader.

DAILY and WEEKLY.

JOHN E. KRAFT.   JOHN W. SEARING.

277 Wall Street,

KINGSTON, N. Y.,

Dec. 3, 1894.

Mr. H. G. Young,

Albany, N. Y.

Dear Sir--

In accordance with your approval of our tunnel under Railroad Avenue and the West Shore tracks, I inclose copies of consents of the Cornell Estate and the U. & D. RR. to the same, for your signature. Will you kindly send them to me as soon as possible.

I appreciate greatly your explanation of your letter in reference to the West Shore elevated structure, in relieving me from the charge of misleading you.

Thanking you for your good wishes, I am

Yours Truly,

John E. Kraft,
Receiver.

[Source: Collection of Eugene Dauner]

For and in consideration of one dollar and other good, valuable and lawful consideration, I do hereby give and grant my consent to the Colonial City Electric Railway Company, a street railway corporation organized under the Act of the Legislature of the State, known as the Railroad Law of 1892, and the acts amendatory thereof and supplemental thereto, to construct, maintain and operate a street surface railroad through upon and along Thomas Street from Broadway to a point opposite such lot or lots as said Company now has or may hereafter acquire between Thomas Street and Railroad Avenue and from thence by tunnel underneath said Railroad Avenue and the right of way tracks and lands of the West Shore Railway Company, to private lands on the easterly side of said West Shore Railway said tunnel to be constructed in a manner approved by the West Shore Railway Company.

And I expressly give and grant my consent to the said Railway Company to operate its said road by electricity and for this purpose the overhead electric system known as the "Trolley System" may be used by the said Company: and I further expressly grant to the said Company the right to erect and maintain the necessary poles and wires for the operation of the said system. IN WITNESS WHEREOF, I have hereunto set my hand and seal this   day of December in the year one thousand eight hundred and ninety-four.

[Source: Collection of Eugene Dauner]

Uptown—Downtown; Horsecars—Trolley Cars

78-4-'95-1,000.

Copy

ULSTER AND DELAWARE RAILROAD COMPANY.

STONY CLOVE & CATSKILL MT. R. R.,
KAATERSKILL RAILROAD.
} NARROW GAUGE DIVISION.

OFFICE OF THE PRESIDENT.

S. D. COYKENDALL,
PRESIDENT.

Rondout, N. Y., Dec. 14, 1896.

To the Mayor of the City of Kingston,

Kingston, N. Y.

Dear Sir:-

You will please take notice that pursuant to a resolution and authority of the Common Council of the City, we placed a crossing on The Strand, in the City of Kingston, over the tracks of the Colonial Traction Company, under the supervision of the City Engineer and Street Committee, on Saturday last, December 12th, 1896, after the Colonial Traction Company had ceased running their cars, and that the same was torn up over the street on Sunday evening without any authority, and that we shall look to the City for all damages sustained and insist that the City replace the crossing at once.

Yours, &c.,

S D Coykendall

President of the Ulster & Delaware R.R

[Source: Collection of Eugene Dauner]

TO THE ASSESSOR OF THE CITY OF KINGSTON:
The Kingston City Railroad Company, a street railway company, duly organized under the Laws of the State of New York, and operating a trolley road in the City of Kingston, N.Y., hereby represents that it is the owner of real estate in the City of Kingston, Ulster County, N.Y., said property being briefly described as follows: It consists of a single track trolley road in two parts; one being from North Front Street, in said City of Kingston, to the Rhinebeck & Kingston Ferry, in said City, being about 2. miles, and another part, separated from the above described part, beginning at the end of the Ulster & Delaware Railroad Company's trestle, and runs through to Kingston Point, being about *one* miles in length, and that the two parts are connected by operating over the tracks of said Ulster & Delaware R.R. That said Company also has a car-house situate on the corner of Broadway and Chester Street in said City of Kingston, and their real estate consists of the tracks, structures for trolley wires and feed wires.

That said real estate is assessed on the assessment roll of the City of Kingston for 1898 at a valuation of $100,000, which valuation is incorrect, and this applicant specifies the respect in which said assessment is incorrect as follows and asks that it may be corrected accordingly, to wit: The property assessed includes the Kingston Point Park which is not owned by the Kingston City Railroad Company but is owned by Samuel D. Coykendall, and that property should be stricken from the assessment against said Railroad Company. The valuation of the real estate of said Company does not exceed $50,000; and such assessment is also incorrect in that the said property is assessed at a greater rate than the Colonial Traction Company's road, located in said City, which has a greater number of miles, and is assessed for $20,000.

That said corporation is not assessed in the manner provided by law.
Dated, Aug. 26th., 1898

S D Coykendall
President

Ulster County, ss: Samuel D. Coykendall, being duly sworn, says that he is the President of the above named Corporation, and that the foregoing statement is true.

[Source: Collection of Eugene Dauner]

Appendix E - Colonial City Receiver's Financial Report

Sep. 23, 1895. The annual report of the receiver of the Colonial City Electric Railway Company for the year ending June 30 last shows as follows:

Gross earnings $11,863
Operating expenses 20,920

Net deficit $9,057
Fixed charges 425
Deficit for year.............. $9,482

The salaries of the general officers and clerks for the year were $1,434, and of the other employees $7,978. The amount expended for fuel was $1,982 and for insurance $296.
[Source: Kingston *Daily Freeman*, September 23, 1895.]

Appendix F - Judge Parker's Injunction Vacation

SUPREME COURT - ULSTER SPECIAL TERM
Kingston City Railroad Company vs Colonial City Electric Railway Company
Application on behalf for an injunction pendente lite, to restrain defendant from crossing Broadway in the City of Kingston.
A. T. Clearwater for plaintiff.
J. Newton Fiero and A. S. Newcomb for defendant.
Parker J.
The defendant having constructed and put in operation within the limits of the city of Kingston nearly six miles of street surface railroad, which it operates by the electric system of overhead wires, commonly known as the trolley system, proposes to cross Broadway diagonally or obliquely from Thomas to Cedar Streets.
Thomas Street does not cross Broadway, and the street nearest Thomas, intersecting with Broadway on the opposite side, is Cedar. The distance from the corner of Thomas Street to a

point on Broadway opposite the corner of Cedar , is 135 feet, as appears from the affidavit of the defendant's engineer.

The defendant having first obtained the consent of the municipal authorities, and of a requisite number of property owners adjoining its proposed route, intends to make the crossing as a necessary step towards connecting the two ends of the route now operated in sections, thus creating a continuous through line from one extreme end of the city to another. Upon Broadway the plaintiff is and for a long time has been lawfully operating a street surface railroad, and it insists that the proposed crossing is in violation of section 102 of the railroad law, and therefore the plaintiff should be enjoined from making it. So much of the section as is necessary to present the question involved reads as follows: "No street surface railroad corporation shall construct, extend or operate its road or tracks in that portion of any street, Avenue, road or highway in which a street surface railroad is or shall be lawfully constructed, except for necessary crossings, without first obtaining the consent of the corporation owning and maintaining the same, except that any street surface railroad company may use the tracks of another street surface railroad company for a distance not exceeding 1,000 feet, whenever the court, upon application for commissioners, shall be satisfied that such use is actually necessary to connect main portions of a line to be constructed as an independent railroad."

Plaintiff's contention is that to cross obliquely from Cedar to Thomas s is without his consent, and is contravention of the provision quoted. A similar statute has been in force since the enactment of chapter 282 of the laws of 1884, but a diligent search on the part of counsel and court has not led to the discovery of a case where this question has been passed upon.

In the matter of Thirty-fourth Streetrailroad company (102 N. Y., 343) the constitutionality of a provision of the street surface railroad law of 1884, of which the one quoted above, is a substantial reenactment, was under consideration. In that case three-fifths of the route of the defendant was proposed to be constructed in streets then occupied by other street railroads and the court, in naming the three precedent conditions to defendant's right to construct and operate its road, gave the third as "the consent of the companies having coincident routes" (page 349). And again at page 352 the court says "the legislature by the act of 1884 in substance determined that it was inexpedient to permit a competing street railroad to be constructed on the line of another road unless the existing road should consent," i. e. should not be constructed "without the consent of roads occupying coincident lines."

As that court was not called upon to consider the question in connection with such facts as are now before the court, its observations on the subject can not be said to have the binding force of authority. But they are of value because they indicate that it was the view of the court that it was the intention of the legislature to protect a street railroad, not from general competition by other street railroads, but from competition on the same street.

The railroad act was passed to facilitate, not to obstruct railroad enterprises, and this fact should be borne in mind in constructing such of its provisions as contain limitations intended for the protection of existing railroads.

That the object of the provision is to protect an existing street railway from loss by competition on and along a street upon which its railroad is operated, and not to subserve a general public interest, is shown by the fact that if the railroad in occupation consent, the would-be competing railroad may parallel its lines any distance.

It is evident, therefore, that the legislature had in view in creating the limitations provided by the section under consideration, the protection not of the general public, but of a surface railroad in actual occupation of a street.

That it was to save such corporation from harmful competition on such street, and that only, is further shown by the fact that the provision quoted expressly provides "that any street surface railroad may use the track of another street surface railroad company for a distance not exceeding 1,000 feet (in cities of the population of Kingston such distance was increased to 1,500 feet by laws of 1894, chap. 693, whenever the court upon an application for commissioners shall be satisfied that such use is actually necessary to connect main portions of a line to be constructed as an independent railroad, and that the public convenience requires the same, in which event the right to such use shall only be given for a compensation to an extent and in a manner as ascertained and determined by commissioners to be appointed by the courts, as is provided in the condemnation law.

How could the legislature more strongly manifest that the intention of the provision is not to obstruct, but merely to protect a surface railroad from the competition of a coincident line on the same street?

It says to a corporation, such as this plaintiff, if it be necessary to connect main portions of a line to be constructed as an independent railroad, it shall have, without your consent, and in spite of your refusal, the use of your tracks for 1,500 feet. But you shall be protected because of such competition and compensated for the use of your tracks by an award the amount of which shall be ascertained and determined by commissioners. Again, the act expressly authorizes crossings to be made, and as it does not provide that the crossings shall be made at a right angle or at any given angle, it would seem to be within the limits of a proper construction of the statute to hold that a crossing may be made at any angle which the peculiar situation of the streets may require.

A different situation would be presented if for any part of the distance the lines should parallel each other, for then the railroad in occupation would likely have a right to insist that for such distance its tracks should be used, and be compensated therefor.

But in this case the distance is so short that the defendant has no use for the plaintiff's tracks; it cannot possibly compete with plaintiff for business on that street, for no one would get on the cars at Thomas to ride diagonally across the street to Cedar, the two streets being separated by a distance of only 135 feet, and defendant does not propose to parallel any portion of plaintiff's line, but to make an oblique from Thomas Street to Cedar.

If the distance between Cedar and Thomas s was so much greater than it is to prevent crossing at an angle for the entire distance, but under 1,500 feet, the defendant could not be prevented from connecting its lines of railroad at those streets, but to accomplish that result it would be obliged to acquire the use of plaintiff's tracks in the manner provided by the statute. But owing to the short distance between such streets, and the extreme width of Broadway at the point of the proposed crossing, it is neither necessary nor desirable to use plaintiff's tracks or parallel them, and therefore it would seem that the defendant proposes to make such crossing as a reasonable construction of the statute authorizes.

Assuming, however, for the purpose of the argument, that the position is not well grounded, still other difficulties confront the plaintiff on this motion.

The plaintiff and defendant entered into a contract on the 24th of January, 1894, which in terms provides for a crossing on Broadway at Thomas and Cedar Streets, and if this argument be binding, the plaintiff cannot avail itself of the statute even if it be capable of the construction for which its counsel contends.

Appreciating this situation, the plaintiff has since the granting of the preliminary injunction, served a supplemental complaint, in which it sets up the contract accompanied by allegations to the effect that the contract is not such as the parties agreed upon and intended to make; that the real agreement of the parties, upon which their minds met, was that the crossings should be from Cornell to Cedar , not from Thomas to Cedar, as expressed in the agreement.

The execution of a different contract than that agreed upon, is alleged to have been due to the mutual mistake of the parties, and its reformation is prayed for. In other words, the plaintiff in effect , says that it executed the contract and is bound by it, unless it can get it reformed, but as it proposes to ask for and claims to be entitled to a reformation by judgement, the court should assume that it will be successful and enjoin the other party to it from proceeding in accordance with the terms.

This position might be tenable if the facts stated by it were not put in issue by the answer which also alleges other facts leading to deny plaintiff's rights to the relief sought. But the equities alleged as a ground for reformation, being put in issue by the answer, "the plaintiff must be content to await the reformation of the contract before it can have affirmative relief based upon the contract as reformed." Allison Brothers Company v. Allison 7, N.Y. Supp. 268.

But were the rule not established that when a plaintiff seeks to have the contract reformed, an injunction upon the basis of it as reformed, should not be granted pendente lite, the plaintiff would encounter the still further difficulties that defendant's answer not only challenges the issuable facts averred in the complaint, but alleges such acts as the parties and surrounding facts and circumstances as in the absence of evidence, permitting contrary inferences of facts to be drawn, would by the way of equitable estopped prevent the plaintiff from obtaining a reformation of the contract although it be true that its execution in its present form was due to a mutual mistake of the parties.

It is true that plaintiff has had no opportunity to traverse such allegations of fact and may be able on a trial to do so successfully, but the possibility that it can do so is not available in its behalf on this motion.

The injunction should be vacated for still another reason often expressed in the books, but rarely better than by Mr. Justice Learned in N. Y. & Albany R. R. Co. v. The West Shore R. R. Co. (11 Abb. New Cases, 880), in which case the affidavits in support of plaintiff's motion tended to show that the two routes were substantially coincident at several points. Said the Court, "there are several reasons why in my judgement this motion should be denied. First, it is a motion for the same injunction which is sought by the judgment asked for in the complaint (Code Civ. Pro. Sec 605). It is not an injunction which is necessary in order that the final judgment may be effectual, (Code Civ. Pro. Sec 604, Subd. 1). And the consideration of this motion involves in fact the trial of the case upon affidavits. Now it is a salutary rule that such an injunction should not be granted, except there be the greatest need therefor. Unless some immediate and irreparable injury will otherwise be done which can not be remedied by the final judgment, the plaintiff should wait until the cause shall be tried."

I see no such immediate and irreparable injury here. If the final judgment shall establish the plaintiff's rights as it claims them, the work which may be done by the defendants between this time and the time of such judgment cannot injure the plaintiff so far as I can see. (Troy & Boston R. R. Co. v Boston H. T. & W. R. R. Co., 18 Hun. 60)., while on the other hand if an injunction should now be granted, and the final judgment should deny the plaintiff any relief, the injury to the defendant would plainly be great and difficult to compute.

To the same effect are Steele vs Pittsburgh & L. E. R. R. Co., 12 N.Y., Supp.576 and Grill vs Wiswall, 82 Hun. 281.

On this motion the same injunction is sought for which judgment is asked in the complaint. And it does not appear that irreparable injury will result if the plaintiff be compelled to wait until the suit shall be tried. The complaint alleges that plaintiff will suffer irreparable injury, but no facts are shown in support of the allegation.

If the defendant makes the crossing, and later on shall be compelled by judgment to take it up, the damage resulting to the plaintiff will be inconsequential. And again it does not appear that plaintiff's property will be damaged more by the crossing proposal than by other crossings made to which it has assented to the contract.

For the reasons given, the motion for an injunction pendente lite should be denied, and preliminary injunction vacated with costs of motion.

Appendix G - Directors of the Colonial City Railroad Company

1896	1897	1899	1900
August Belmont	John N. Cordts	August Belmont	August Belmont
Abram Hasbrouck	Abram Hasbrouck	John N. Cordts	John N. Cordts
Gilbert D. B. Hasbrouck	Gilbert D. B. Hasbrouck	Abram Hasbrouck	Abram Hasbrouck
George Hutton	George Hutton	Gilbert D. B. Hasbrouck	Gilbert D. B. Hasbrouck
William Hutton	William Hutton	George Hutton	George Hutton
John E. Kraft	John E. Kraft	John E. Kraft	John E. Kraft
Charles M. Preston	Alva S. Newcomb	Luke Noone	Alva S. Newcomb
William F. Russell	Luke Noone	Charles M. Preston	Luke Noone
John I. Waterbury	Charles M. Preston	John I. Waterbury	Charles M. Preston

Appendix H - Special Policemen

A. E. Benson, John Keefe, John Lounsberry, Jared Francisco, James Murphy, Charles Frazier, John . . ., Albert Mays, George Schick, John Rafferty, A. W. Belcher, John D. Schoonmaker, George Saulpaugh,

Urban Transportation in Kingston, New York, 1866-1930

Thomas Hickey, Joseph A. Coen, Roswell Saulpaugh, Daniel Herrick, Stewart Benson, John Phelan, Norman Conner, Charles Moore

Appendix I - Plans and pictures of the Colonial Subway
From *Street Railway Journal*, December 1899

Above:
Entrance to Colonial City subway from West Shore station.

Right:
Steps to Colonial City subway platform.

Below:
Side elevation and plan showing method of supporting West Shore Tracks.

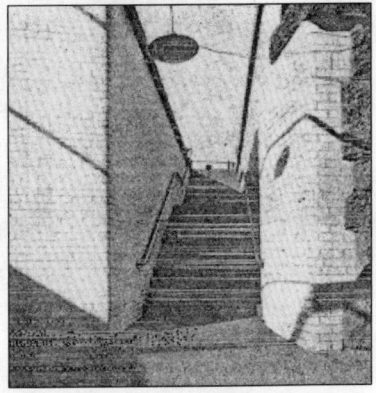

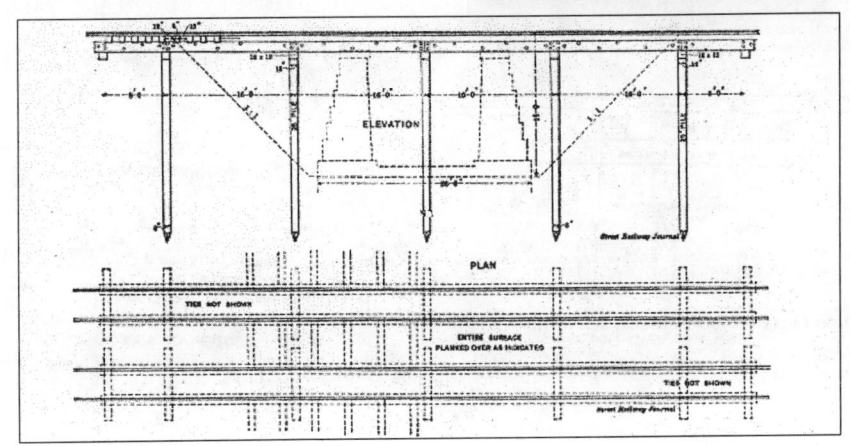

Uptown—Downtown; Horsecars—Trolley Cars

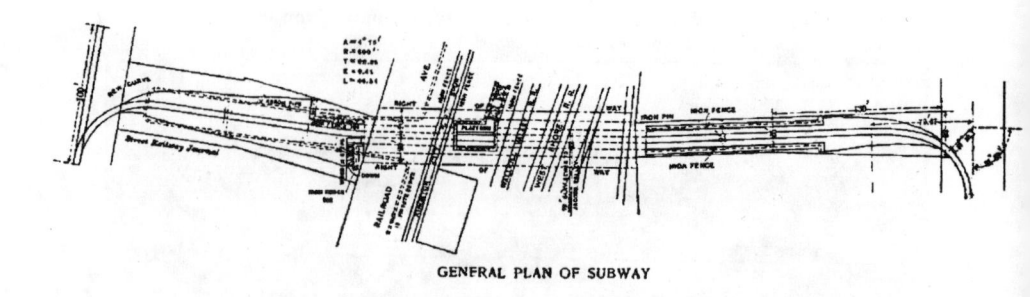

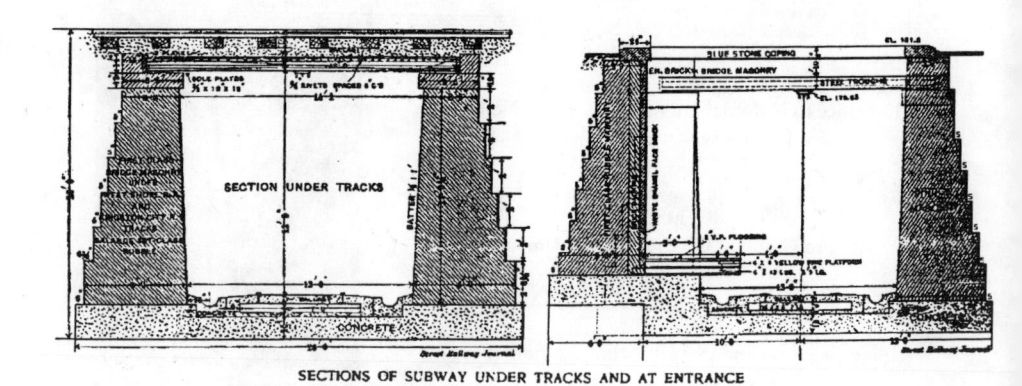

GENERAL PLAN OF SUBWAY

SECTIONS OF SUBWAY UNDER TRACKS AND AT ENTRANCE

SECTION OF TEMPORARY STRUCTURE FOR SUPPORTING STEAM RAILROAD TRACKS

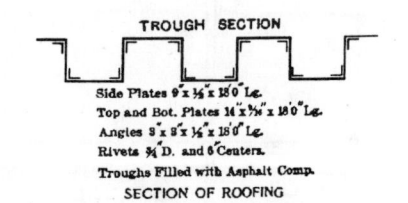

TROUGH SECTION

Side Plates 9" x ½" x 15'0" Lg.
Top and Bot. Plates 14" x 7/16" x 15'0" Lg.
Angles 3" x 3" x ½" x 15'0" Lg.
Rivets ¾" D. and 6" Centers.
Troughs Filled with Asphalt Comp.

SECTION OF ROOFING

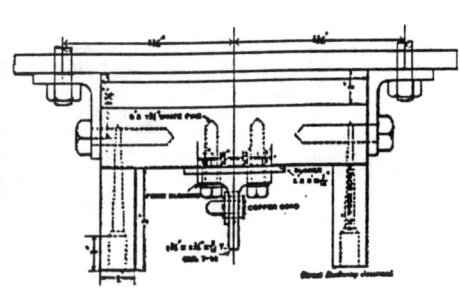

URBAN TRANSPORTATION IN KINGSTON, NEW YORK, 1866-1930

Left: Entrance to subway. Right: Original method of attaching conductor to roof.

Appendix J - Colonial Subway Details

A very interesting piece of construction work, by which a five-track grade crossing with a steam railroad was avoided, has recently been completed by the Colonial City Traction Company, of Kingston, N. Y. The work is unique so far as is known in the history of small electric railways in the country, for the Colonial City Traction Company owns only 14 cars, and may be an important suggestion to other companies placed under somewhat similar conditions.

The circumstances which led up to the construction of this subway were as follows: The city of Kingston is intersected by the West Shore Railroad, and possessed up to a few years ago but one railway company {Kingston City Railroad Company}, whose line crossed the railroad tracks on grade at right angles. The Colonial City Traction Company was organized as a competing line. Franchises were secured and about two miles of track were built on each side of the city down to the crossing. An effort was then made to secure the right of crossing the West Shore tracks on the tracks of the existing company for a distance of 800 feet, but this was refused by the latter company. The Colonial City Traction Company then (in 1896) went to the Supreme Court for privilege to condemn the right of way over these tracks, and won the suit. The case was appealed, however, by the existing railway company, and carried to the Appellate Division of the Supreme Court, which decided that the consent of the municipal authorities and of the abutting property owners were prerequisites to the action, in this way reversing the decision of the lower court. The question was then carried up by the new company to the Court of Appeals, which sustained the last decision. The Colonial City Traction Company then secured the permission of the authorities but were unable to obtain that of the property owners. Under these circumstances a request was made to the Appellate Division to appoint commissioners to decide whether the property owners for these 800 feet were unreasonable in withholding their consents; the commissioners found in favor of the new road. These suits created much interest at the time, as deciding important legal questions, and were commented upon in an extended way in the STREET RAILWAY JOURNAL. During the final litigation, however, a compromise was reached between the two railway companies, by which the Colonial City Traction Company, instead of crossing the West Shore tracks on the tracks of the existing company, agreed to divert its route a short distance to the north, and build a subway under the West Shore tracks, thus connecting its two existing sections.

The covered part of the subway is 220 feet in length, with approaches of 130 feet on the east side and 160 feet on the west side. The sides of the subway under the West Shore Railroad tracks are of first-class bridge masonry, and elsewhere are first-class rubble masonry. The subway station is faced with white enameled brick; the roofing is of open-hearth steel troughs, with a tensile strength of 60,000 pounds per square inch. The plates and angles composing the troughs of the solid floor system were covered with asphalt, mixed ten parts asphalt and 30 parts coal tar pitch. The bottoms were then filled with a binder composed of one-quarter inch clean, sharp gravel and No. 4 asphalt paving composition in the proportion of 1 cubic foot of gravel to 1 gallon of paving composition. There is an entrance to the subway from the platform of the West Shore Railroad Company. This has proved a great convenience to passengers and a means through which the company has greatly added to its traffic, as will be described later. The entrance to the West Shore station is fitted with handsome hand-rails of heavy brass pipe of two inches in diameter, and all stone work is of North River blue stone.

Work on the subway was commenced August 22, 1898, and the first car ran through it on March, 19, 1899. The work was carried on without any delay to traffic on the West Shore Railroad. The method of supporting the tracks on the latter is illustrated on this page (see Appendix H). Before any excavation was made within the West Shore right of way a temporary trestle was constructed by driving 25 foot piles between the tracks. These piles were white oak and not less than eight inches on the top and 12 inches diameter at the butt. After being driven they were capped by 12 inch by 12 inch yellow pine caps, secured to the piles by wrought iron drift pins 1 inch square and 22 inches long. On these caps were laid the track stringers , which were of yellow pine 8 inches by 16 inches, and long enough to cover two bents in the trestle. Two stringers were placed under each rail and decked with cross ties. The entire deck was then covered with 2 inch yellow pine plank. This supported the tracks while the excavation for the subway was being made.

The method of conducting current to the cars in the subway was another problem, and that first employed is illustrated in section. It consisted of T iron, two and one quarter inches by two and one quarter inches by five-sixteenths inches thick, lag-screwed to an 8 inch by 1 and three-quarter inch white pine plank, which was held to the roof girders by angles. The plank protected on the edges by 1 inch by 3 inch timbers, held to the upper plank by wood screws, making a trough to catch the trolley in case it should jump from the conductor. A rubber cushion 3 inches by 3 inches by 3/16 inches was used between the conductor and the trough. This construction proved, however, to be too rigid and noisy, in spite of the precautions taken to prevent trouble of this kind, and has since been changed to ordinary trolley wire carried on hangers.

Before the subway was completed and during its construction passengers were transferred from one section of the road to the other, across the West Shore tracks, by bus. The completion of the subway was naturally followed by large increase of traffic, partly because the line was now a continuous system and also partly because its proximity to the only railway station in the city. As a result, the gross receipts of the company have increased 75 per cent during the past six months, as compared with the corresponding period a year ago. The entire cost of the subway was about $28,000.

The system of the Colonial City Traction Company has interesting features besides the subway. As Kingston has a population of only about 30,000, and there are two lines in the city, the keenness of competition put forth every effort to secure as much traffic as possible. Considerable popularity has been secured by the Colonial City Traction Company through the opening of its subway. Another step to secure traffic was the introduction of cross-seat cars, which proved very popular. The amount of traffic did not require long cars, so the experiment was tried of using cross-seats in an 18 foot closed car. There are six seats on a side, and a view of one of these cars, which were built by the Pullman Company is illustrated (in Appendix H). The company has in all seven closed and six open cars, mounted on Peckham and Diamond trucks. G. E.-800 motors are used under the former and Westinghouse 49 motors under the latter. The open cars are of the ten-bench type, and were built by Jackson & Sharp.

Colonial City sprinkler car.
Courtesy The Trolley Museum of New York

Another novelty in car construction is the sprinkler car. This was gotten up by the superintendent of the company, C. Gordon Reel, at a cost of $65, and consists of a large barrel holding 1600 gallons, purchased of a local brewer for $10, and mounted on a platform car. The cost of the sprinkler, fittings, etc., which were all homemade, brought the cost up to that stated. In winter this car is fitted with nose plow and used as a snow plow.

The power station is located at the eastern end of the line on the Hudson River, and contains two 150-h.p. Ball & Wood tandem compound condensing engines belted one to a 125-kw. and one to a 150-kw Westinghouse generators; the two generators are run in parallel. The condensers and pumps are of the Worthington type, and there are two Sterns tubular boilers of 300 h.p. each. Eighty-pound girder rails are used. The improvements described had an excellent effect on the increase in traffic of the railway.

The road is now in the hands of and operated by a reorganization committee consisting of John I. Waterbury, Charles M. Preston and August Belmont, with C. Gordon Reel as superintendent. Mr Reel was formerly connected with the Lindell Railway, of St. Louis, but assumed control of the Kingston road in November 1896. The receipts have increased 75 per cent during the last year, with an increase in car mileage of 15 per cent and a decrease in operating expenses over 1898 of $6,000 (from $35,000 to $29,000). The cars are now earning about $20 a day on an average of 15 hours each. The electrician of the company is C. J. McNelis, and Francis Gaffney is the chief engineer of the power station.

[Source: *Street Railway Journal*, pp 861-864, December, 1899.]

Appendix K - Directors of the Kingston Consolidated Railroad Company

1905	1906	1907	1910
August Belmont	August Belmont	August Belmont	Hewitt Boice
Hewitt Boice	Hewitt Boice	Hewitt Boice	A. N. Day
A. M. Day	A. M. Day	Howard Chipp	Abram Hasbrouck
Abram Hasbrouck	Abram Hasbrouck	A. M. Day	George Hutton
Gilbert D. B. Hasbrouck	Gilbert D. B. Hasbrouck	Abram Hasbrouck	Fred T. Ley
George Hutton	George Hutton	George Hutton	Harold A. Ley
Luke Noone	Augustus J. Phillips	Augustus J. Phillips	J. C. Page
Augustus J. Phillips	Charles M. Preston	Charles M. Preston	Augustus J. Phillips
Charles M. Preston		C. Gordon Reel	

Appendix L - Kingston Consolidated Rule Book

Kingston Consolidated R. R. Company

STANDARD CODE
OF
RULES
FOR THE GOVERNMENT OF
CONDUCTORS AND MOTORMEN

ALL EMPLOYEES WHOSE DUTIES ARE PRESCRIBED BY THE RULES WILL BE FURNISHED WITH A COPY, FOR WHICH THEY WILL SIGN A RECEIPT, AND WILL BE REQUIRED TO HAVE THE BOOK IN THEIR POSSESSION WHILE ON DUTY

KINGSTON, N. Y.:
PRINTED BY R. W, ANDERSON & SON,
1905.

INDEX

	Page
Knowledge of Rules	3
Report for Duty	3
Personal Appearance	3
Politeness	3
Habits and Personal Conduct	4
Responsibility	4
Talking to Motorman	5
Safety	5
Standing on Steps	5
Stealing rides	5
Ejectments	
Eject, Where to	5
Intoxication	6
Run on Time	6
Fire in Car	6
Reporting Defects	7
Disabled Cars	7
Assistance, Render	7
Medical Attendance	7
Accidents, Fatal	7
Accidents, Reports to be Full and Complete	7
Accidents, Report to Officials	8
Information, Give to Proper Persons	8
Telephone Information	9
Signals, Bell	9
Signals, before passing Obstructions near Track	10
Signals, Starting	10
Signals, Danger	10
Leaving Car	11
Responsibility for damages	11
Transfer Point Meetings	11
Hearing by Superintendent	11

Uptown—Downtown; Horsecars—Trolley Cars

RULES FOR CONDUCTORS -		RULES FOR MOTORMEN -	
Be on Rear Platform	11	Stopping for Passengers	13
Announcements	11	Churches and Hospitals	14
Removing Trolley	12	Persons Between Cars	14
Carrying Packages	12	Passing Standing Cars	14
Watching the Trolley	12	Passing Vehicles	14
Moving Forward	12	Fire Apparatus	14
Seating Passengers	12	Ambulance and Police Patrol	14
Assisting Passengers	12	Reversing Cars	14
Spitting on Floor	12	Leaving Car	15
Collection of Fares	13	Throwing Overhead Switches	15
Change	13	Power Off Line	15
Register Rings	13	Current, Economical Use of	15
Register out of Order	13	Release Brakes before Stops	16
Transfers in Blockades	13	Water on Tracks	16
		Sanded Tracks	16
		Spinning of Wheels	16
		Slippery Rail	16
		Do Not Oil Car	16

Kingston Consolidated R. R. Company

STANDARD CODE OF RULES
for THE GOVERNMENT OF
CONDUCTORS AND MOTORMEN

1. KNOWLEDGE OF RULES - Conductors and motormen are required to be familiar with the rules, and with every special order issued. The bulletin board must be examined daily for special orders. Employment by the Company binds the employee with the rules and regulations, and ignorance thereof will not be accepted as an excuse for negligence or omission of duty. If in doubt as to the exact meaning of any rule or special order, application must be made to the office for information and explanation. In addition to these rules, special orders will be issued from time to time; such orders, when issued by proper authority, whether in conflict with these rules or not, must be observed while in force.

2. REPORT FOR DUTY - Regular conductors and motormen must report for duty five minutes before leaving time for their first trip, or if for any good reason unable to report, must give ample notice before such leaving time. Extra men must report at such time as ordered.

3. PERSONAL APPEARANCE - Conductors and motormen must report for duty clothed in full regulation uniform, and must be clean and neat in appearance.

4. POLITENESS - Conductors and motormen must treat all passengers with politeness, avoid difficulty, and exercise patience, forbearance and self-control, under all conditions. They must not make threatening gestures or use loud, uncivil, indecent, or profane language, even under the greatest provocation.

5. HABITS AND PERSONAL CONDUCT - The following acts are prohibited:

5a. Drinking intoxicating liquors of any king while on duty.

5b. Entering any place where the same is sold as a beverage while in uniform or while on duty, except in cases of necessity.

5c. Constant frequenting of drinking places.

5d. Carrying intoxicating drinks about the person while on duty.

5e. Carrying intoxicating drinks on the Company's premises at any time.

5f. Indulging to excess in intoxicating liquors at any time.

5g. Gambling in any form, including the laying of bets (and playing raffles) while upon the premises of the Company.

5h. Smoking tobacco while on duty.

5i. Smoking tobacco while off duty in any part of the Company's buildings, except in the conductors' and motormen's room.

5j. Reading books or newspapers while on duty.

6. RESPONSIBILITY - The motorman is in charge of the car and is held responsible
  (1) For the safe running of the car.
  (2) For the proper operation of the car and its machinery.
  (3) For running car according to schedule.

The conductor is in charge of the passengers on the car and is held responsible
  (1) For the safety and convenience of the passengers.
  (2) For the collection and proper accounting of fares.

7. TALKING to MOTORMEN - Motormen while operating cars are permitted to answer questions of superior officers, and to give proper instructions to students only. All other conversation with motormen while car is in motion is forbidden.

8. SAFETY - The safety of passengers is the first consideration. All employees are required to exercise constant care to prevent injury to persons or property, and in all cases of doubt take the safe side.

9. WARNING TO PASSENGERS - Conductors and motormen must, in a polite way, endeavor to keep people from jumping on or off cars while in motion. If persons attempt to get on or off the car while it is moving, they should be notified politely to wait until the car stops. If the passengers are leaving while another car is approaching from the opposite direction, they should be courteously warned to look out for the car on the other track.

10. STANDING ON STEPS - Do not permit anyone to stand on the steps or buffers. Passengers should be fully inside of car before the signal is given to start.

11. STEALING RIDES - Any person caught stealing a ride on a car must never be pushed therefrom while it is in motion.

12. EJECTMENTS - Ejectments shall be made with the assistance of the motorman after the car has been brought to a stop, using only such force as is sufficient to expel the offending passenger with a reasonable regard for his personal safety.

13. WHERE TO EJECT - Any person ejected from a car must be put off at a regular stopping place.

No passenger will be put off at a point where likely to be exposed to danger.

Particular attention must be paid to this rule during bad and inclement weather, late at night, or when a passenger is intoxicated.

14. INTOXICATION - No passenger will be ejected from a car for mere intoxication, unless said passenger becomes dangerous or offensive; such passenger must then be ejected with great care and must be guided until free from probable injury.

15. RUN ON TIME - Cars must never be run ahead of schedule time, but must pass time points and leave terminals promptly on time, unless unavoidably delayed.

16. STEAM RAILROAD CROSSINGS - Cars must be brought to a full stop at a safe distance, approaching steam railroad crossings at grade, and motorman must not proceed until conductor has gone ahead to the center of crossing, looked both ways, and given the **COME AHEAD** signal. Before starting, the motorman will look back to see that no passengers are getting on or off; and in no case proceed, even after conductor's signal, until he has also examined the crossing and satisfied himself that steam cars are not approaching.

Where there is more than one track the conductor must remain in advance of the car until the last track is reached.

After boarding car, conductor will give **GO AHEAD** signal to notify motorman that he is aboard. Motorman is forbidden to proceed without this signal.

Where crossing is protected by derail interlocking plant, or flagman, this rule does not apply, special instructions being issued to govern in such cases.

17. FIRE IN CAR - When there is evidence of car being on fire, motorman will immediately throw overhead switch to **OFF** and conductor pull down trolley, both motorman and conductor using every effort to prevent passengers becoming panic-stricken or leaving car before it is brought to a stop.

18. REPORTING DEFECTS - Conductors and motormen will report to superintendent, inspector, starter or foremen any defect in car, track or wire, which needs immediate attention.

19. DISABLED CARS - The motorman or conductor of any disabled car, withdrawn from the main track, must remain with the car until relieved by proper authority.

20. RENDER ASSISTANCE - In case of accident, however slight, to persons or property, in connection with or near any car, the motorman and conductor in charge of the same will render all assistance and practicable. In no case will they leave injured persons without first having seen that they are cared for.

21. MEDICAL ATTENDANCE - Motormen and conductors are directed not to employ medical attention to injured persons, except for the first visit, in case of personal injury; nor will they visit such persons at any other time afterward, unless specially instructed so to do by an officer of the Company.

22. FATAL ACCIDENTS - In the event of a fatal accident, it will not be necessary to blockade the line awaiting the arrival of the coroner or any other official. If an accident occurs where it is impossible to carry the body to a place of shelter and security, motorman and conductor will put the body on the car and convey it to some suitable place.

23. REPORT TO BE FULL AND COMPLETE - A full and complete report of every accident, no matter how trivial, and whether occurring on or near the car, must be made by the conductor. Accidents sometimes considered as not worth reporting are often the most serious, troublesome and expensive.

The conductor will obtain the name and residence in full of all witnesses on or near the car.

The motorman will assist the conductor in securing the names of witnesses whenever practicable, and will be held responsible for any neglect to render assistance.

In all cases full facts must be obtained and stated in reports as follows:

The date, exact time, exact place, run and car number, and the direction in which the car was moving, the nature of the accident or collision, and the cause of its occurrence.

The full name and address of the person injured or whose vehicle was in collision (giving the full name of both the driver and owner of the vehicle).

Ascertain the extent of injuries or damage, if any, before leaving the spot.

In case a person is struck by a car after passing around the rear of a standing car, the numbers of both cars must be obtained, and both crews must report the accident.

If an accident is caused by any defect or damaged condition of car, conductor must report the

24. REPORT ACCIDENTS TO OFFICIALS - Conductors and motormen will make a verbal report to the first official of the Company they meet of any accident, blockade or mishap of any kind.

25. GIVE INFORMATION TO PROPER PERSONS - No employee shall, under any circumstance, give any information whatever concerning any accident, delay, blockade or mishap of any kind to any person except a properly authorized representative of the Company.

26. TELEPHONE INFORMATION - In case of accident involving personal injury or serious damage to property, conductor will telephone at once to headquarters, giving notice and particulars of accident.

In case of blockade, where assistance is required to get cars moving, conductor of first car in block must perform this duty. Expense of telephone message will be refunded upon application at office.

27. BELL SIGNALS - From conductor to motorman, to be given on motorman's signal bell:

1 bell - **Stop at next crossing or station.**
2 bells - **Go ahead.**
3 bells - **Stop immediately.**
4 bells (given when car is standing) - **Back car slowly.**

From motorman to conductor, to be given on conductor's signal bell:

1 bell - **Come ahead.**
2 bells - **Watch the trolley** and danger signal to conductor.
3 bells - **Set rear brake.**
4 bells - Signal to conductor that motorman desires to back car.
5 bells - Warning - **Pull trolley down to roof.**

Whenever a car in service is stopped, the motorman will, as soon as he is ready to go forward, give two taps of the gong; after which if the conductor is ready to proceed, he will give the **GO AHEAD** signal.

The motorman will answer the signal to stop from the conductor by one loud tap of gong; and two loud taps of gong after receiving the signal to go ahead .If unable to proceed immediately upon receipt of signal motorman will wait for another **GO AHEAD** before starting the car.

When the car is standing, and motorman desires to back, for any reason, he will give the conductor four bells, but must not move the car until the conductor has answered with four bells to signify **All is clear behind.**

29. SIGNALS BEFORE PASSING OBSTRUCTIONS NEAR TRACK - Before passing any vehicle or obstruction close to the track, where passengers or conductor are liable to be injured while standing on the step of an open car, motorman must give two taps of signal bell as a warning, and must bring his car to a full stop before passing vehicle or obstruction unless he has received **GO AHEAD** signal from the conductor indicating that all is clear. Great care must be exercised in passing over all excavations, warning workmen of the approach of car by repeatedly sounding gong, car to be under full control. Where excavations are near regularly stopping place, car should be run clear thereof before stopped.

30. STARTING - Motorman must never move car (whether stopped on signal or for any other reason) without signal from conductor, and then only when assured that no one is getting on or off front platform.

Conductor must never give signal to start when passengers are getting on or off.

Conductor must never give signal to back a car unless he is on the rear platform and knows track is clear behind the car.

31. DANGER SIGNALS - Red lights or flags indicate danger, and when placed on the track, cars must come to a full stop until such signal is removed.

32. LEAVING CAR - When necessary for conductor to leave his car he must notify the motorman to protect passengers and car. Should passengers board car during absence of conductor , motorman will notify conductor of the number and location of such passengers upon his return.

Cars in commission must not be left unprotected; either conductor or motorman always remaining in charge.

33. RESPONSIBILITY FOR DAMAGES - Employees will be held responsible for any damages caused by their neglect or carelessness or by disobedience of rules.

34. TRANSFER POINT MEETINGS - Motormen and conductors will be held equally responsible for leaving a transfer point so quickly as to prevent the transfer of passengers from an approaching car on a connecting line.

35. HEARING BY SUPERINTENDENT - A hearing will be given by the superintendent to every employee who desires to complain. Reports of suggestions for the betterment of the service will always receive consideration/

RULES FOR CONDUCTORS

101. BE ON REAR PLATFORM - Remain on rear platform when not collecting fares, keeping a lookout for persons desiring to board car. Keep careful watch of passengers to observe requests to stop car. When stops are made at principal streets, places of amusement, churches, or at any other point where a considerable number of passengers enter or leave the car, conductors should be on rear platform until such point is passed.
102. ANNOUNCEMENTS - Announce distinctly the names of streets, public places and transfer points when approaching the same.
103. REMOVING TROLLEY - Do not remove trolley from wire at end of run, or elsewhere at night, until passengers have alighted from car.
105. CARRYING PACKAGES - Passengers must not be allowed to carry bulky or dangerous packages aboard cars.
 Do not in any way take possession of, or assume responsibility for, any package which a passengers may bring upon the car, excepting such articles as are to be turned into the Lost Article Department.
 Do not hang nor allow articles to be hung on the brake handles.
106. WATCHING THE TROLLEY - Keep your hand upon the trolley rope when passing over switches, crossings, or going around curves. Should the trolley leave the wire the conductor must at once pull down the trolley and signal the motorman to stop. After the car has stopped, replace the trolley on the wire, look around and through the car and see if any persons are boarding or leaving same before giving motorman signal to start. See that passengers keep their hands off the trolley rope.
108. MOVING FORWARD - On closed cars when standing passengers crowd the rear door, request them to **PLEASE STEP FORWARD**.
109. SEATING PASSENGERS - Standing passengers should be directed to vacant seats; and an effort made to provide them with seats where possible.
110. ASSISTING PASSENGERS - Elderly and feeble persons, women and children should be given assistance getting on and off car when possible.
112. SPITTING ON THE FLOOR - No passengers will be ejected from a car for spitting on the floor. If a passenger violates the rule or law prohibiting spitting, the conductor will call the attention of the passenger to the law forbidding such conduct, and endeavor to persuade the passenger to desist.
113. COLLECTION OF FARES - Fares must be collected promptly after passenger has boarded car and immediately registered. When more than one person boards car at a time, the fares must be registered immediately in the presence of the passenger who paid them before any more fares are collected.
114. CHANGE - When necessary to give change, first register fare, and immediately thereafter give change.
115. REGISTER RINGS - Be careful to see that register rings each fare and that the dial shows it.
116. REGISTER OUT OF ORDER - In case the register gets out of order, stop using it, make report of fares on back of trip report or on blanks supplied for that purpose, and report the fact.
117. TRANSFERS IN BLOCKADES - In case any line is blocked, it is the desire of the Company to carry passengers to their destination on other lines. Under such circumstances conductors of parallel or intersecting lines will accept transfer tickets accordingly and will issue a transfer on a transfer if necessary. They will also accept transfer passengers without tickets on orders from any official or authorized representative of the Company making report of same on back of trip report.

RULES FOR MOTORMEN

201. STOPPING FOR PASSENGERS - Keep a careful lookout on both sides of the street and bring the car to a full stop for every person who signals except that when a car has considerable headway, is overcrowded, and another car follows within the same block (or 200 feet) passengers should be requested to take the following car.
 Cars will stop on signal at farther corners; at car stations, transfer points, and at points as provided in special orders.
 Do not stop so as to block cross streets or cross walks.
202. CHURCHES AND HOSPITALS - When passing a church during the hours of service, and at all times when passing a hospital, run slowly and do not ring the gong unless necessary.
203. PERSONS BETWEEN CARS - Cars moving in opposite directions must not pass at points where persons are standing between the tracks, but must be operated so as not to occupy both tracks at such point simultaneously.

Uptown—Downtown; Horsecars—Trolley Cars

204. PASSING STANDING CARS - When passing standing cars gong must be rung and car brought to slow speed.

205. PASSING VEHICLES - Motormen are cautioned to exercise great care when a vehicle is passing alongside of track ahead of car. Ring the gong vigorously to attract the attention of the person driving, as a warning not to pull in ahead of car; and run cautiously until the vehicle is passed in safety.

206. FIRE APPARATUS - When any fire department vehicles are observed approaching from any direction, cars must be stopped until such vehicles have passed.

207. AMBULANCE AND POLICE PATROL - Ambulances and police patrol must be allowed the right of way, and when approaching or passing, cars must be kept under control to avoid collision.

209. REVERSING CARS - Never use the reversing lever to stop car except to avoid a collision or injuring a person or animal, or when the brake rigging is disabled.

Do not reverse the power when the brake is set, but release the brake and reverse the power simultaneously, and when the reverse lever is thrown in position, apply the current one point at a time, otherwise the fuse will melt of the breaker will release. Sand should be used when making an emergency stop.

210. LEAVING CAR - Never leave the platform of car without taking reverse handle, throwing off the overhead switch and applying brake. Be careful to see that the hands point to the **OFF** mark before taking off the controller handle.

Before leaving car at any point, set hand brake sufficiently to prevent car from drifting.

211. THROWING OVERHEAD SWITCHES - An overhead switch must not be thrown until power is turned entirely off, except in case controller cylinder fails to turn power is on. It must be thrown by hand only.

212. POWER OFF LINE - When the power leaves the line, the controller must be shut off, the overhead switch thrown, and the car brought to a stop; the light switch must be turned on and the car started only when the lights burn brightly.

213. ECONOMICAL USE OF CURRENT - In order to effect an economical use of the electric current, it is necessary that the continuous movement of starting and increasing speed should be made gradually. In starting a car, let it run until the maximum speed of each notch has been attained before moving handle to the next notch.

Do not apply brakes when the current is on,.

Do not apply current when brakes are applied.

Do not allow the current to remain on when car is going down grade, or when passing over section breakers. Endeavor to run car with the least amount of current, allowing the car to drift without the use of the current when it can be done without falling behind time.

A great amount of power can be saved by using judgment and discretion in approaching stopping places and switches by shutting off the power, so as to allow the car to drift to the stopping place or switch without a too vigorous use of the brake.

214. RELEASE BRAKES BEFORE STOPS - When brakes are set to make a stop they should always be released, or nearly so, just before the car comes to a standstill.

215. WATER ON TRACK - When there is water on the track, run the car very slowly, drifting without use of power whenever possible.

216. SANDED RAILS - Never run on freshly sanded rails with brakes full on except to prevent an accident.

217. SPINNING OF WHEELS - Care must be taken particularly during snow storms, to avoid **spinning** of the wheels with no forward or backward movement of the car.

218. SLIPPERY RAIL - On a slippery rail do not allow wheels to slide; as soon as wheels commence to slide, the brake must be released and reset.

Extreme caution must be used to keep car under full control approaching all intersections, junctions, railroad crossings and prominent driveways, being very careful when approaching wagons and other cars, disregarding schedule if necessary.

219. DO NOT OIL CAR - Do not oil or grease any part of a car.

Appendix M - Kingston Consolidated Inspection

October 25, 1907. I made an inspection of the Kingston Consolidated Railroad and submitted the following report:

This system consists of 7.91 miles of single track, all located in the City Of Kingston and on public streets, except where one line is carried under the West Shore railroad for a distance of 616 feet and where the same line enters the property of the company at Kingston Point Park for a distance of 410 feet.

On the line there are eight crossings of steam railroad tracks, six at grade, one under and one over. The maximum grade on the line is 9 percent.

The company owns, available for operation, 38 cars. Of these, 14 are closed and 24 are open. Of the closed cars, 6 are 16 feet; 6 are 18 feet; and 2 are 22 feet inside measurements. All closed cars are heated by electric heaters, and are equipped with screen vestibules. Of the open cars, 6 are 10 bench, and 18 are 9 bench. All cars have single chain brakes and are equipped with sand boxes. The closed cars have 33 inch and the open cars 30 inch chilled wheels., 2 1/2 inch tread, and 5/8 inch flange. Cars weigh from 9 to 12 tons.

The company has 16 G.E. 800 motors; 5 were put in service in 1892, 3 in 1894, 4 in 1895, 1 in 1896 and 3 in 1899; also 10 G. E. 1,000: 1 was put in service in 1893, 4 in 1895, 1 in 1896, 4 in 1899. In addition to the above, the company has one combination sprinkler and snow plow equipped with 2 G.E. 800 motors. The company's power house is located on East Strand at the foot of Abruyn Street, near the Rondout Creek. It is equipped with two 150 hp. tubular boilers, 100-lb. steam pressure; two 306 hp. Babcock & Wilcox water tube boilers, 150-lb. steam; two 150 hp. Ball & Wood tandem compound condensing engines, belted to two 125 kw Westinghouse generators; and two 300 hp. Ball & Wood engines direct connected to two 200kw. Westinghouse d.c. generators. The plane was enlarged in 1901-2, and is equipped with a new marble switch board, new piping, heaters, pumps, condensers, etc., throughout. All current is d.c. 575. The company has sufficient feeder for operation purposes.

During the season of 1907 new, hard center crossings have been laid at the track intersections at Main and Fair Streets and at St. James Street and Clinton Avenue; 2,932 feet of 80-lb. girder and 72-lb. grooved rail have been replaced by 90-lb. standard T rail in 60 foot lengths on the Strand and Ferry Street. Work is now in progress replacing 1,701 feet of these same girder and grooved rails on Broadway, Main Street and Fair Street. A gang of about thirty men has been employed on this work, and 2,591 ties have been used, Four thousand five hundred feet of new trolley wires have been installed this year, and at present the entire overhead structure is being renewed on the Colonial division from East Strand to the terminus at Kingston Point, a distance of 3,335 feet.

A force of ten men during the day and three men at night is employed in cleaning, inspecting and repairing cars. At night, every car which has been in service during the day is swept and sprayed with a sanitary solution. As occasion requires, the outside bodies are washed. During the past year every car was inspected throughout including a complete overhauling of the motors, brakes and truck equipment, after which overhauling each car was painted and varnished. This is in line with the practice of the company, which is to thoroughly overhaul, repair, paint and varnish every closed car during the summer months and every open car during the winter months.

All cars are housed in the company's barn at Broadway and Chester Street, which is ample in size to hold the company's entire equipment. It is equipped with pits for inspection, a complete steam heating plant, an isolated paint shop, a boring mill, a wheel press, a lathe and drill press and other tools, all of which are electrically driven and sufficient for the company's requirements to come.

The company has a most recent type of sand drier located in the car barn where sand is dried, after which it is stored at convenient points for use on the cars.

The company has blanks on which records are made of defects and repairs to car equipment.

The company operates two lines of cars, one the Colonial division, the other the Kingston City division. The cars of the Colonial division are run from Marius Street to Kingston Point, a distance of 5,241 miles. These cars run from Marius Street through Washington Avenue, through North Front Street from Washington Avenue to Wall Street, through Wall Street from North Front Street to Main Street, through Main Street from Wall Street to Clinton Avenue, through Clinton Avenue from Main Street to Cedar Street, through Cedar Street to Broadway, across Broadway to Thomas Street, through Thomas Street to Subway, through Subway to Dederick Street, through Dederick Street to Prince Street, through Prince Street to Hasbrouck Avenue, through Hasbrouck Avenue to East Strand, through East Strand to North Street, through North Street to Delaware Avenue, through Delaware Avenue to Kingston Point Park terminus. It takes 35 minutes to make the run, and seven cars are operated on 10-minute headway from 8 a.m. to 9 p.m. and on 20-minute headway from 6 a.m. to 8 a.m., and 9 to 12 p.m.

The regular number of crews during the year is eighteen. During the summer months about ten or twelve more regular crews are employed. In addition to these men a number of extra men are employed throughout the year, but principally during the summer months. The plan of the manager is to recruit such extra new throughout the city as have employment during the day.

The company does no freight or express business. No foreign cars are handled. Mail is carried on regular cars. Maximum number of passengers carried for one day was 24,242 during the past season. In addition to the sand boxes on the cars, a sanding car is operated during bad weather. The foreman of the shop is held responsible for the condition of sand boxes on cars. The company has a book of rules and a schedule is posted in the car barn.

On Broadway, there is a grade descending towards the ferry terminus commencing at St. Mary's church and extending to the Strand, a distance of 1,886 feet. This grade is continuous, with a maximum of 7.6 percent. On this grade there is an easy curve with another near the foot. Near the top of the grade there is a turnout switch, and all cars are obliged to run slow to take the switch just before coming to the grade. On the Colonial division, on Hasbrouck Avenue, there is a heavy grade from Delaware Avenue to St. Mary's Street, a distance of 1,238 feet. This grade descends toward Kingston Point. and the maximum grade at any point is 9 percent. There is one curve of medium radius something less than half way down the hill, with a tangent at the foot. A bulletin posted instructs motormen in case of doubt as to the safety of operation on either of these grades not to proceed down them.

Kingston Point Park is a popular summer resort. The company owns about forty acres of land on which a number of buildings are located, including a large refreshment pavilion, merry-go-round, bowling alleys, photograph gallery, summer houses, terminal office etc. Except upon special occasions, no admission fee is charged to the park. No intoxicating liquors are sold on the grounds. There is a shelter station at this point equipped with gates, which are used to restrain the crowds from boarding the cars after the trolleys and seats have been turned for the return trip, and in this manner separating the in-coming from the out-going passengers. During the season of heavy travel to and from this park, both lines of cars are operated to and from the park. In addition to the regular schedule, extra cars are run, no trailers being used. The distance between the junction of the two lines at the Ferry and the park is about 6,652 feet. When extras are run, they are fed in as the traffic requires. No signals are carried. No oil tail-lights are used.

At the junction of Hasbrouck Avenue and Prince Streets the single electric track crosses the single track of the Ulster and Delaware railroad at grade. This is a special work crossing with the steam rail cut; in fair condition. The electric track is on a curve and the steam track on a tangent; both are level. On the south side of the crossing the view of the steam track to the east is obstructed, and a view to the west can be had for 500 feet. On the north side the view is unobstructed in either direction. The crossing is protected by a flagman from 7 a.m. to 6 p.m. This crossing should be equipped with a derail in the electric track on the south side of the crossing, and a metal trough should be placed on the trolley wire.

On Hasbrouck Avenue the single electric track crosses the single track of the Ulster and Delaware railroad. This is a special work crossing, with the ball of the steam rail cut. It is in fair condition. The steam track is on a curve and the electric track on a tangent. This crossing is at the foot of a long grade on the west side of the crossing, and at the foot of a light grade on the east side. The steam track being on a curve, the necessary elevation makes it impossible to maintain a smooth riding crossing at this point. This condition also adds to the possibility of derailment on the crossing. On the west side of the crossing, a view of the steam track to the north can be had for 1,000 feet, and to the south for 300 feet. On the east side a view to the north can be had for 500 feet, and to the south the view is limited. This crossing is protected by a flagman from 7 a.m. to 6 p.m. This crossing should be equipped with a derail in the electric track on the east side, and a metal trough placed on the trolley wire extending over the crossing. No suggestion is made for a derail on the west side of the crossing on account of the possibility of accident caused by it to runaway cars on the long, heavy grade on that side. This crossing is known as the Murray Street crossing.

On Hasbrouck Avenue the single track of this company crosses the single track of the Ulster and Delaware railroad at grade. This is a diagonal crossing, with special work, in fair condition. The ball of the steam rail is cut. The approach to the crossing on the east side is up a grade for 250 feet, with a maximum of 8 percent. On this approach there are short sections of rail which are loose and in poor condition. On the west side the track is practically level. The steam track is on a curve and the electric track on a tangent. The elevation necessary in the steam track results in a poor condition of the crossing on the electric track. The view is limited in each direction on either side of the crossing. This crossing is protected by a flagman from 7 a.m. to 6 p.m. This crossing should be equipped with a derail in the electric track on the west side of the crossing, and a metal trough placed on the trolley wire. Also the short sections of rail in the electric track should be replaced by proper construction.

On the Strand the single track crosses a switch track of the Ulster and Delaware railroad. Only switching movements are made on the steam track. This is a diagonal cut crossing in fair condition. On account of the character of traffic on the steam track, no suggestion is made for derails at this point.

On the Strand the single electric track crosses the single track of the Ulster and Delaware railroad. This is a diagonal cut crossing, the ball of the steam rail cut. It is in good condition. Both tracks are level and nearly straight. The steam track extends to the day boat line. There are two passenger trains daily during the summer season, and some switching is done year round. On the east side of the crossing the electric track is parallel and along side the steam track. The view is open and clear. On the west side the view is obstructed. On account of the character of traffic on the steam road, and the method of operation at this point, except that during the season when the steam trains are operated, cars on the electric track bound for the park should come to a stop and the conductor go ahead and flag over the crossing.

On Broadway the single electric track crosses two main line tracks of the West Shore and one main line of the Wallkill Valley railroad. This is a cut crossing with special work in good condition. The West Shore depot is located about four hundred feet north of the crossing. The crossing is protected by gates operated from a tower at all hours. I am informed that arrangements have been made for placing a metal trough on the trolley wire extending over this crossing. No further suggestion is made for protection at this point.

Nearly all of the track of the Kingston City division which is constructed of girder rail is in poor condition, except that portion on the garde on Broadway. Work is at present being done replacing this rail, and I am informed that it is the intention of the company to entirely replace it with 100 pound T rails as fast as the work can be carried on.

The track of the Colonial division, which consists mostly of 7 in. 80-lb. girder rail, is in fair condition, but not first class, and I am informed that it is the intention of the company to renew all of this rail within the next two years.

The cars of the company are in good condition; clean, comfortable, and well painted. The company has sufficient power for maximum requirements of operation.

The dangerous features in the operation of this road are the heavy grades and the grade crossings of steam railroad tracks. Proper care is taken in the operation of the heavy grades. The brake equipment is considered sufficient for the class of cars operated.

To increase the safety of operations on this railroad the following recommendations are made:

That the Public Service Commission, Second District, State of New York, order the Kingston Consolidated Railroad Company, as follows:

1. That the crossings of its tracks with the single track of the Ulster and Delaware railroad at the junction of Hasbrouck Avenue and Prince Street it places a derail switch in its track on the south side of the crossing, this derail to be operated by conductors of electric cars from a point near the steam track, and that it places a metal trough in the trolley wire extending over this crossing.

2. That at the crossing of its track with the single track of the Ulster and Delaware railroad on Hasbrouck Avenue, known as Murray Street crossing, it place a derail switch in its track on the east side of the crossing, to be operated by conductors of electric cars from a point near the steam track, and that it piece a metal trough on the trolley wire extending over this crossing.

3. That at the crossing of its track with the single track of the Ulster and Delaware railroad on the Hasbrouck Avenue it place a derail switch in its track on the west side of the crossing, to be operated by the conductors of electric cars from a point near the steam track, and that it place a metal trough on the trolley wire extending over the crossing. Also that the short sections of rail in the electric track on the west side of the crossing be replaced by proper rail construction.

4. That during the season when steam cars are operated, cars bound for the park come to a stop, and conductors go ahead and flag over the crossing of the Ulster and Delaware railroad as suggested in the body of this report.

5. That the above recommendations be completed within six months from the acknowledged receipt of the order.

A copy of this report was transmitted to the vice-president and general manager of the company, who replied that the company would comply with all the recommendations; and later, reported that the derails had been installed, and other progress.

Appendix N - Kingston Consolidated Financial Reports

Jan. 10, 1905. QUARTERLY REPORT OF KINGSTON CONSOLIDATED RR CO. FOR QUARTER ENDING DEC. 31, 1904

	1904	1903
Gross Earnings	$27,964	$27,700
Operating Expenses	15,754	17,015
Net earnings	12,210	10,685
Other income	150	
Gross income	12,210	10,835
Fixed charges	10,147	9,874
Net income	2,062	961

The general balance sheets shows as follows:

ASSETS
Cost of road and equipment ... $1,112,020
Supplies on hand 2,820
Due by companies and individuals ... 765
Cash on hand 1,052
Prepaid insurance 391
Total $1,117,054

LIABILITIES
Capital stock................. $ 400,000
Funded debt 700,000
Interest on funded debt........... 2,291
Due for wages..................... 700
Due for supplies 382
Profit and loss................. 13,681
Total..................... 1,117,054

[Source: Kingston Daily *Freeman*, January 10, 1905.Apr. 15, 1905.]

QUARTERLY REPORT OF KINGSTON CONSOLIDATED RR CO.
FOR QUARTER ENDING MAR. 31, 1905

	1905	1904
Gross Earnings	$22,716	$23,466
Operating Expenses	15,578	16,752
Net earnings	7,138	6,714
Other income	150	150
Gross income	7,288	6,864
Fixed charges	9,857	10,101
Net loss	2,569	3,237

The general balance sheets shows as follows:

ASSETS
Cost of road and equipment	$1,112,341
Supplies on hand	2,320
Due by other than agents	694
Cash on hand	2,052
Prepaid taxes	1,795
Prepaid insurance	1,882
Total	$1,121,084

LIABILITIES
Capital stock$	400,000
Funded debt	700,000
Interest on funded debt	7,666
Due for wages	591
Due for supplies	1,714
Profit and loss	11,113
Total	1,121,084

[Source: Kingston *Daily Freeman*, April 15, 1905.Oct. 7, 1905.]

QUARTERLY REPORT OF KINGSTON CONSOLIDATED RR CO.
FOR QUARTER ENDING September 30, 1905

	1905	1904
Gross Earnings	$42,268	$41,466
Operating Expenses	23,449	23,716
Net earnings	18,819	17,750
Other income	150	50
Gross income	18,969	17,800
Fixed charges	9,806	10,136
Net income	9,163	7,664

The general balance sheets shows as follows:

ASSETS
Cost of road and equipment	$1,115,041
Supplies on hand	2,127
Due by companies and individuals	1,030
Cash on hand	5,542
Prepaid taxes	1.086
Prepaid insurance	708
Total	$1,125,534

LIABILITIES
Capital stock	$400,000
Funded debt	700,000
Interest on funded debt	7,625
Due for wages	828
Due for supplies	1,363
Profit and loss	15,718
Total	1,125,534

[Source: Kingston *Daily Freeman*, October 7, 1905.Jan. 10, 1906.]

Quarterly report - December 31, 1905

	1905		
Gross Earnings	$126,357.55	Fixed charges	39,431.31
Operating Expenses	74,313.74	Net income	13,212.50
Net earnings	52,043.81	Dividend	8,000.00
Other income	660.00	Surplus	5,212.50
Gross income	52,643.81	Surplus brought forward	13,680.93
		Total surplus	18,893.43

The surplus of %5,212.50 is $2,845.53 greater than 1904. During the year 2,590,701 passengers were carried. 66,859 transfers were issued. The miles traveled amounted to 534,816 with earnings of 23.65 cents per mile and operating expenses of 13.9 cents.
[Source: Kingston *Daily Freeman*, January 10, 1906.Nov. 3, 1906.]

URBAN TRANSPORTATION IN KINGSTON, NEW YORK, 1866-1930

QUARTERLY REPORT OF KINGSTON CONSOLIDATED RR CO.
FOR QUARTER ENDING SEP. 30, 1906

	1906	1905
Gross Earnings	$49,130	$42,268
Operating Expenses	22,557	23,449
Net earnings	26,573	18,819
Other income	150	150
Gross income	26,723	18,969
Fixed charges	9,950	9,806
4 per cent div, pfd stock	8,000	8,000
Net income	8,773	1,163

The general balance sheets shows as follows:

ASSETS		LIABILITIES	
Cost of road and equipment	$1,116,304	Capital stock	$400,000
Supplies on hand	8,685	Funded debt	700,000
Due by companies and individuals	1,076	Interest on funded debt	7,625
Cash on hand	13,720	Due for wages	751
Prepaid insurance	1,640	Due for supplies	1,917
Prepaid taxes	993	Profit and loss	32,125
Total	$1,142,418	Total	1,142,418

[Source: Kingston *Daily Freeman*, November 3, 1906.Aug. 11, 1919.]

Street Railway Operating at Loss Under 6-Cent Fare

Notwithstanding increased revenues from six-cent fares, the Kingston Consolidated Railroad Company operated at a new loss of $1,908 during the quarter ending June 30, 1919., according to a report submitted by the traction company to the Public Service Commission Second District, State of New York.

	1918	1919
Railway operating revenues	$39,762	$46,960
Railway operating expenses	25,621	37,912
Net operating revenue	14,141	9.048
Taxes assignable to railway operations	2,536	2,597
Operating income	11,605	6,451
Non-operating income	210	139
Gross income	11,816	6,590
Interest on funded debt	8,489	8,438
Interest on unfunded debt	271	60
Total deductions from gross income	8,760	8,498
Net corporate income or loss	3,056	(1,908)

[Source: Kingston *Daily Freeman*, August 11, 1919.Nov. 18, 1919.]

The report of the Kingston Consolidated Railroad Company for the quarter ended Sep. 30, as made to the Public Service Commission,. Second District, shows a net profit of $9,381. If this were a fair average a years net income would be over $37,000, but the quarter just reported is probably the most profitable of any as it included the heavy summer traffic. The six-cent fare was put into operation for one year, the Public Service Commission having power to put the company back on a five-cent basis after that period.

The report follows:

Railway operating revenues	$61,606	Non-operating income	50
Railway operating expenses	40,711	Gross income	$17,993
		Deductions from gross income:	
Net operating revenues	$20,895	Interest on funded debt	$ 8,534
Taxes assignable to railway operations	2,952	Interest on unfunded debt	60
Operating income	$17,943	Other deductions	18
		Total deductions from gross income	$ 8,612
		Net Corporate income	$ 9,381

[Source: Kingston *Daily Freeman*, November 18, 1919.]

May 9, 1921. The Kingston Consolidated Railroad Company, for the quarter ended March 31, 1921, operated at a net loss of $2,146, as shown by its report to the Public Service Commission. A marked improvement over the corresponding quarter in 1920, is shown, however, when the loss was $5,328. This year the operating revenue showed a substantial increase while the operating expenses were decreased nearly $1,500. Interest on the funded debt, as usual, made the biggest hole in the revenue, amounting to $8,076, and deductions not itemized were $2,235 this year against $754 in 1920.

This is one of the company's "lean" quarters., travel being the smallest of the year. The condensed profit and loss statement compiled by the commission from the company's report for the two quarters follows:

	1920	1921
Railway operating revenues	$48,384	$51,002
Railway operating expenses	42,086	40,605
Net revenue, railway operations	6,298	10,397
Net Operating revenue	6,228	10,397
Taxes assignable to railway ops	2,698	2,707
Operating Income	3,600	7,790
Gross income	3,600	8,240
Interest on funded debt	8,100	8,076
Interest on unfunded debt	75	75
Other deductions	754	2,235
Total deductions from gross income	8,929	10,386
Net corporate loss	5,328	2,146

[Source: Kingston *Daily Freeman*, May 9, 1921.Jul. 21, 1924.]

For the six months ending June 30, 1924, the Kingston Consolidated Railroad Company carried 235,381 revenue passengers less than for the same period in 1923, according to the financial report submitted to the public service commission at Albany this month.

The report shows that during the first six months in 1923 the trolley road lost $3,384 while for first six months of this year the loss amounts to $15,619.

The report filed with the public service commission is given below in condensed form so that it may be more easily understood.

	1924	1923
Revenue	$95,999	$111,456
Expenses	84,298	86,678
	$11,701	$24,778
Taxes	7,360	7,698
	4,341	17,080
Interest charges etc.	19,960	20,464
Total loss	15,619	3,384

[Source: Kingston *Daily Freeman*, July 21, 1924.Dec. 17, 1924.]

The report of the Kingston Consolidated Railroad Company, as filed with the public service commission for the nine months period beginning Jan 1, 1923 and Jan 1, 1924 to September 30, 1923 and September 30, 1924, respectively shows that both the operating revenues and operating expenses decreased in 1924, but while expenses were reduced $5,029 from the corresponding period of 1923 the operating revenues during the same period were reduced $16,633. While the company showed a net corporate income for the nine months period of 1923 of $2,346; a net corporate loss of $9,246 is shown for the same period in 1924. The results of the company's operations during the two periods is shown as follows:

	01/01/23 - 09\01/23	01/01/24 - 09/30/24
Railway operating Revenue	$169,588	$152,955
Railway operating exp	129,027	123,998
Net Revenue	40,561	28,957
Taxes assignable to railway operations	11,367	11,659
Operating income	29,195	17,299
Non-operating income	3,444	3,940
Gross income	32,638	20,339
Deductions from Gross Income		
Int on funded debt	20,800	19,950
Int on unfunded debt	3,037	3,330
Other deductions	6,455	6,305
Total deductions	30,292	29,585
Net Corp inc/loss	Inc 2,346	Loss 9,246

[Source: Kingston *Daily Freeman*, December 17, 1924.]

Appendix O - Kingston Point Park Lease

1. This was the leasing price mentioned.
2. Open at all times for trolley cars and park to be in operation from May 30 to and including Labor Day from 7 a.m. 12 p.m. with man in charge of park to help facilitate operation of cars. Use of telephone.
3. Maintain all buildings and fixtures including the big pavilion and toilets on dock, and painting, carpentering, etc. Park to be turned back in as good as when turned over and no alterations to buildings and lawns without railroad's consent.
4. Shrubs, trees and foliage to be trimmed annually. Lawns and edges to be kept cut and in proper condition. Paths and walks to be kept free from ruts.
5. All privilege leases to expire when park turned back to railroad.
6. Park to be policed and no liquor to be sold on premises.
7. Driveways through park not to be made a general driveway for taxicabs and autos.
8. Railroad to furnish current for lighting and operation of merry-go-round.
9. City not to sub-let park.
10. Cancel city's lease with three months notice.

Appendix P - Skip Stop System Stops

KINGSTON CITY DIVISION STOPS

North Front and Wall	Post Office
John	Armory at special functions
Main	O'Reilly
Pearl	Library
St. James and Fair	Foxhall
Clinton	Chester
St. James and Broadway	Delaware
Elmendorf	Chestnut
Van Buren and Downs	McEntee
Henry and O'Neil	Spring
Cedar and Cornell	Abeel
Railroad	Strand

Special stop at Broadway and Ferry at beginning and close of work at boat yards.

Hasbrouck	Rhinebeck Ferry

STOPS ON COLONIAL DIVISION

Marius	Cedar and Clinton
Warren	Sterling
Pearl	Broadway and Cedar
Main	Thomas and Broadway
Lucas	Subway stairs
N Front & Washington	Post Office
Crown	Hasbrouck and Garden
North front and Wall	Foxhall
John	Chester
Main and Wall	Delaware
Fair	Newkirk
Clinton and Main	Murray de-railer
Maiden Lane	Meadow
St. James	Mill de-railer
Franklin	Strand and Hasbrouck
Henry	Ferry
Lindsley mill crossing	

Special stops between Lindsley mill and Ferry Streets at beginning and close of work at boat yards and railroad shops.

Sycamore	Hart's Corner
Abruyn	Park Oste
Union	Park

Appendix Q - Bus Routes Replacing Colonial City Trolley Cars

The uptown belt line route starts at Cedar Street and Broadway, goes up Broadway to O'Neill , to Foxhall Avenue, to Albany Avenue, to Clinton Avenue, to North Front , to Washington Avenue, to Linderman Avenue, to Wall , to Henry , to Clinton Avenue, to Cedar, to Broadway.
The running time of the busses over the above route is half an hour and busses will run in each direction. Beginning Wednesday morning the first bus leaves Cedar Street and Broadway at six o'clock, making the complete round trip and arriving at Cedar Street and Broadway at 6:30 o'clock.
At 6:45 o'clock another bus starts in the opposite direction so that every fifteen minutes a bus will leave Cedar Street and Broadway after 6:30 o'clock in the morning.
A bus will also pass the junction of Clinton Avenue and John Street every 15 minutes, the being the center of the route covered.
Two buses will be operated to take care of the travel on the belt line route until 9:15 o'clock at night, after which only one bus will be on that route.

The Kingston-Rondout route starts from St. Joseph's church at main and Wall s to Clinton Avenue to Henry, to Broadway, to Prince, to Hasbrouck Avenue, to Delaware Avenue, to Murray, to Hasbrouck Avenue, to Strand, to Broadway, to Ferry, to Hasbrouck Avenue, and return uptown over the same route.

This bus service starts at 6:10 a.m. from each end of the route and a bus will then leave from each end at twenty minute intervals, and will continue running until 11:50 p.m., when the bus from each end of the route will run to the car barn.

Busses going downtown from Main and Wall s leave that corner every 10, 30, 50 minutes after the hour.

Busses going downtown pass the corner of Sterling and Henry Streets every 15, 35 and 55 minutes after the hour.

Busses going downtown pass Foxhall Avenue and Hasbrouck Avenue every 20 and 40 minutes after the hour and on the even hour.

Busses going downtown pass Delaware Avenue and Murray Street every 5, 25 and 45 minutes after the hour. Busses going uptown leave Hasbrouck Avenue and the Strand every 10, 30 and 50 minutes after the hour.

Busses going uptown pass Delaware Avenue and Murray Street every 15, 35 and 55 minutes after the hour.

Busses going uptown pass Foxhall and Hasbrouck Avenues every 20 and 40 minutes after the hour and on the even hour.

Busses going uptown pass Sterling and Henry Streets every 5, 25 and 45 minutes after the hour.

Appendix R - Proposed Bus Routes - June 19, 1928

Route No. 1 known as the Broadway or through route would begin at Wall and North Front Streets and thence go over North Front to Fair Street, to Pearl Street, to Albany Avenue, to Broadway, to Strand, to Hasbrouck Avenue, to Ferry Street and returning over Ferry Street to Broadway, to Albany Avenue, to Pearl Street, to Wall Street, to North Front and Wall Streets, the place of beginning.

Two busses would be used on this route on twenty minute time from 6 a.m. to 7 a.m. and from 9 p.m. to 12 p.m. On Saturdays the last trip on ten minute time would be at 10 p.m. On Sundays and holidays the twenty minute busses would begin operating one hour later and the ten minute busses two hours later.

Route No. 2, also to be known as the Main Route, would have the following route:

Begin at Wall and North Front Streets to Fait Street, to St. James Street, to Clinton Avenue, to Henry Street, to Broadway, to Prince Street, to Hasbrouck Avenue, to Delaware Avenue, to Murray Street, to Hasbrouck Avenue, to Ferry Street, to Strand, to North Street, to Delaware Avenue, to Kingston Point gate. In winter, when the Day Line boats are not running the route would end at North Street and Delaware Avenue, if thought feasible.

The return route would be over Delaware Avenue to North Street, to Strand, to Ferry Street, to Hasbrouck Avenue, to Murray Street, to Delaware Avenue, to Hasbrouck Avenue, to Prince Street, to Broadway, to Henry Street, to Clinton Avenue, to St. James Street, to Wall Street to North Front and Wall Streets, the place of beginning.

Three busses would be operated on this route on twenty minutes time between upper Kingston and Kingston Point. They would start on Sunday at 7 a.m.

Route No. 3, which is now known as the Belt Route, would remain unchanged, the route being as follows:

Beginning at Cedar Street and Broadway, over Cedar Street, to Clinton Avenue, to Henry Street, to Pine Street, to Greenkill Avenue, to Wall Street, to Linderman Avenue, to Washington Avenue, to North Front Street, to Clinton Avenue, to Albany Avenue, to Foxhall Avenue, to O'Neill Street, to Broadway, to Cedar Street, the place of beginning.

Two busses would be used on this route, as at present, one bus leaving thirty minutes over the route indicated, and another bus leaving every thirty minutes going in the opposite direction.

Appendix S - Trolley Replacement Public Hearing

Alderman-at-large C. Ray Everett, president of the common council presided at the public hearing which had been called by Mayor Dempsey. All of the aldermen were present with the exception of Alderman Joyce who had been excused. The aldermen present were Aldermen Zucca, Haines, Myers, Molyneaux, Sullivan, Mann, Derrenbacher, Doheny, McGrane, Relyea, Schoonmaker, and McCardle.

The large council chamber was well filled with delegations from both the Ponckhockie section and the Clifton Avenue section of the city, who listened attentively while City Clerk Walter H. Gill read the petition from the trolley road.

The executive committee of the Uptown Business Men's Association sent in a petition recommending that the petition of the trolley road be granted as the present bus lines were giving good service.

Urban Transportation in Kingston, New York, 1866-1930

A petition from the Parent Teachers Association of School No. 4 and residents of Ponckhockie asked that the present 10-minute Broadway trolley service be maintained in Ponckhockie and that the trolley road utilize the franchise given it some time ago to operate through Gill Street, Walnut Street, Lindsley Avenue and Delaware Avenue to Kingston Point, returning by way of North Street, Strand and Broadway.

The petition was signed by 227 residents of Ponckhockie.

A petition with 313 signers was read from the Clifton Avenue section of the city asking that the Hasbrouck Avenue bus line be extended over East Chester Street, Highland Avenue, Clifton Avenue, Stephan Street and Foxhall Avenue.

Principal R. H. Van Valkenburgh of School No. 4 was the first to speak. He said that the residents of the Ponckhockie section of the city were very anxious that the 10 minute service be continued. It has been operating a good many years and there was still business enough to warrant its continuance. He said that a 20 minute schedule would work a hardship on the residents in that section and called attention to the fact that six of the members of the school faculty in Ponckhockie used the trolley service every school day. One teacher was forced to leave her home extremely early as it required 55 minutes to reach the school even with the 10 minute schedule on the trolley road. If there was a 20 minute schedule she would have to leave home much earlier. In closing he said that times were progressing but to allow the trolley road to establish a 20 minute service to Ponckhockie school would be retrogressing.

Joseph Netherwood Jr. said that many of the people of Ponckhockie were employed in stores and industrial plants in the upper end of the city, and were not able to walk to work. For that reason he said that Ponckhockie needed the 10 minute service it was now getting and he saw no reason why it should not be continued. He also saw no reason why the trolley road should not utilize the franchise it held covering Gill Street, Lindsley Avenue and other streets in Ponckhockie.

Charles S. Brooks of Walnut Street believed that the present trolley line should be maintained in preference to busses. He said that during the winter the trolley road assisted in opening the streets it ran through of snow, but if they operated busses they would not do so and it would likely mean additional expense to the city in purchasing more snow removal equipment.

Mr. Brooks said that even with the 10 minute schedule when there was a heavy snow storm those who desired to use the trolley cars had to wait longer for a car and with busses operating they would probably have to wait forty minutes.

George C. Kent of Crane Street, the last speaker of the Ponckhockie delegation, said he had heard a lot of talk about the 10 minute service and that there were between five hundred and six hundred voters in Ponckhockie. He said that he had listened to the petition of the uptown business men urging that the trolley road petition be granted and said that if Ponckhockie was given a 20 minute schedule instead of the present 10 minute headway that the residents if they missed a bus would walk to Rondout in ten minutes and do their shopping for that reason he urged the uptown business men to "Get behind us and help us keep the 10 minute service."

In closing he said what Ponckhockie wanted was for the busses to follow the present trolley tracks to Ponckhockie and the 10 minute headway maintained.

E. J. Ritch of Clifton Avenue was the first speaker for the delegation from that section of the city. He said that the uptown section of the city had a good cross town line service and believed that the Clifton Avenue section should have service equally good.

Max Reuben, the real estate operator, said he desired to supplement what Mr. Ritch had said. He said that during 1928 more residences were erected in the Third ward than in any other section of the city. He believed that was true also of 1929. He said that the people of that section were asking for bus service and should receive it.

Former Alderman James T. O'Reilly said that before the common council granted a franchise to the trolley road for a 25 year period the city would receive something in return as the franchise was a valuable one. He said that no one could foretell what would happen in the next twenty-five years and did not favor granting a franchise for too long a time.

Harold Darling of Clifton Avenue also favored bus service for that section of the city. He said that many of the residents of that locality had to walk a considerable distance from their homes before they could reach the bus line or trolley line.

Mr. Myers of 120 Grant Street also spoke in favor of bus service in the Third ward. He said that the Clifton Avenue section had never has bus service and he knew that all of the residents in that locality favored having bus service.

President Everett asked if there were any other present who desired to be heard. No one responded and he declared the hearing closed.Appendix T - Amusement Park

Kingston Consolidated trolley at Propheter's.
Courtesy The Trolley Museum of New York

"Old Trolley Cars Will Grace Mr. Propheter's Amusement Park"

Having outlived their day as a means of transportation, they will shelter fishermen, tourists, hot dogs at Ulster Park. Elaborate plans are made for a new resort.

Now that the Kingston Consolidated Railroad Company has made the change from trolley cars to buses, some persons may be interested to know what became of the trolley cars. All the closed cars and many of the open ones were purchased by John D. Propheter, the owner of Twin Lakes Homestead Farm in Ulster Park. The last of these cars are now being drawn to his farm on the huge lumber trucks of F. A. Waters, the lumberman of Highland Avenue, Kingston, for some of these car bodies weight as much as five tons, and must be hauled to and set down on some seemingly inaccessible places.

Mr. Propheter intends to convert his entire farm of 150 acres, through which both highways run for half a mile, into a sort of amusement park and country vacation complex and to this end he will put all these car bodies to many different uses. Some of them will be made into double, i.e., a well-lighted, airy basement room, the size and shape of the floor of each car body, will be constructed of concrete blocks and stone, and on top of this body will be set, so that the floor of the car will become the ceiling of the basement room, thus doubling the room space.

One of these double-deckers will be used as a public waiting station, with the usual conveniences of such a place, for bus passengers. It will be placed on the northwest corner of the new highway {route 9W} and the center lane leading to the lake.

Another will be used as a watch tower for State Troopers of this section to keep a lookout on this particular mile and a quarter, which on weekends and holidays is traversed by from 20,000 to 30,000 cars, many of which go at dangerous speed, dangerous to the occupants of those cars, dangerous to others in other cars and dangerous to pedestrians using the highway. For this reason the basement room of this Trooper's station will, it is hoped, be equipped with a first aid kit and used as an emergency station for such aid, should that at any time become necessary.

This double-decker will be placed on the southwest corner of the highway and the lane leading to the lake, the most advantageous point from which an unobstructed view may be had of this entire stretch, considered by all who have seen it as offering the greatest inducement to speed maniacs to indulge their dangerous sport.

One of the cars will be fitted up as a Dairy Quick Car, mainly to dispense the dairy products of Mr. Propheter's fine herd of Jersey cows - the highest grade of Jersey milk by the glass or bottle, cream, butter, and cottage cheese. This car will be placed about a hundred yards north of the waiting station.

Several cars will be placed about 60 feet back from the highway, and equipped to accommodate tourists. Sufficient yard space around each of these will be enclosed by a picket fence to accommodate an automobile, and to insure some degree of privacy to the occupants of the car.

Some open, or summer cars, will be placed right on the edge of the 60 foot highway and are to be used as observation cars for those who on holiday wish to see the world roll by them while they are seated comfortably in a safe place.

Some cars will be hidden in clusters of woods in different nooks on the farm for those who like seclusion and solitude. TwO, a closed car and an open car, will be placed on the peak of the hill at the lake from which a fine view may be had of the Hudson river, both lakes, both highways, and all the meadows of the farm.

Some will be placed along the shore of the lake for vacationists and tourists who prefer to be near a body of water on account of the sport it affords. One of these car bodies will be divided into six compartments to be used as dressing rooms for bathers.

Lake Repose, which borders the entire eastern front of the farm, is a beautiful body of water, hidden almost completely from the highway by a heavy fringe of woods encircling its shores. From its northern inlet to its southern outlet, or navigable strait, where it empties into the twin, Mirror Lake, which borders on the eastern front of the Golden Rule Inn, the larger Lake Repose is nearly a mile long, about two-thirds of a mile wide and at many places very deep. It is continuously being replenished and refreshed by many large springs at its bottom.

Both these lakes are under the protection of the State Conservation Department, which fact in itself implies their importance as bodies of water and this Commission annually restocks these lakes liberally with bass, pickerel, wall-eyed pike and perch. Comparatively few persons living in Kingston know of Lake Repose, and hence make no use of it, whereas a great many people from Poughkeepsie and Highland make use of it often during the entire season, camping on its shores, boating, fishing and bathing.

On the whole, this easily accessible farm is a real country-place, which will afford everything that the run of a hundred and fifty acres of meadow, mountain, woods and large bodies of water can give to the lover of outdoor life.

Mr. Propheter intends to lay out a full sized baseball field in the large meadow on the east side of the new highway at the extreme northern part of his farm. The entire field will be made level and rolled with a steam roller. A grandstand with a seating capacity of about seven hundred persons will be improvised with 8 or 10 open trolley cars placed end to end. Each car will have its seats placed lengthwise of the car and will accommodate as many persons as it did formerly in its original role. The roof of each of these cars will be arranged for bleacher benches to accommodate those who, while watching a game of the national sport or other games, can at the same time take sun baths. So that the faithfull old trolleys will not be junked, but be doing double duty next season.

The parking space around the border of the ball field is ample enough to accommodate two hundred automobiles for those persons who prefer watching games or assemblages from the seats of their own cars.

A tennis court will be constructed in the large, south meadow adjoining the ball field.

This farm certainly has within its boundaries a sufficient number of different kinds of twins to justify its name - there are, of course, the twin lakes, connected by a navigable strait, then there are the twin highways, connected by a sort of Siamese link, and the two large gently rolling fields and the lake, constituting twin landing places for land planes as well as water planes.

[Reprinted from the Kingston *Daily Freeman*, October 1, 1930.]

Bibliography

Blumin, Stuart M. *The Urban Threshold* (Chicago and London: The University of Chicago Press, 1976), pp118-119

De Lisser, *Picturesque Ulster* (Styles & Bruyn Publishing Company, 1897)

Kingston, NY Tercentenary - 1652-1952 (Freeman Publishing Company, 1952)

Kingston's 350th Anniversary - 1609-1959 (Catskill Mountain Publishing Corp.)

Rigby Jr., Harry, editor. *Kingston's Bicentennial* (Kingston Bicentennial Commission, 1976)

State of New York; Board of Railroad Commissioners *Eleventh Annual Report of the Board of the Board of Railroad Commissioners of the State* (n.p.:January 8, 1894)

"Subway at Kingston," *Street Railway Journal*, December, 1899 pp 861-864

Kingston Newspapers: *Argus, Daily Freeman, Democratic Journal, Journal, Journal & Weekly Freeman, Leader, Press, Weekly Freeman, Weekly Leader, Daily Freeman*
Rondout Newpapers: *Courier, Daily Freeman, Freeman* (weekly)

Acknowledgments

I would like to thank the following people for their assistance in obtaining reference materials used in this book: Eric A. Fedde; Alfred Marquart; Joseph Fautz; The Trolley Museum of New York; Edward Ford, City of Kingston historian; Roger Mabie; The Friends of Historic Kingston; Eugene Dauner; Alan Adin and Steve Finkle of the City of Kingston and Jon McGrew, William Brandt, Joseph Kluepfel, Evan Jennings and Andy Pecararo of the Trolley Museum of New York.

Index

Abeel Street 34, 72
Abruyn Street 32, 75, 85
Adams
   Campbell W. 60
Albany Avenue 86, 93, 94, 97
Alexander and Green 50
Alger
   Horatio 39
Alliger
   Hasbrouck 57
Atkins
   DuBois G. 50, 82
Atwater
   Robert 12
Auchmoody
   M. O. 82
Balch
   George 61-63
Baldwin
   Elihu J. 12
Ball and Wood Company 33
Ball Engine Company 41
Bankers Trust Company 93, 94
Barnard
   Joseph F. 59, 63, 64
Barnhart
   Hiram 19
Barnes 77
Bauer's Hotel 67
Beadle
   William 79
Bell
   Milton 54
Belmont
   August 56, 59
Benson
   Anthony 19
Benton 78
Bernard
   Reuben 19, 56
Best
   Harry 53
Best
   Hiram 53
Betts
   James A. 82
Block 87-89
Blood
   William H. 45
Bloodgood
   Clarence E 42, 43
Boice
   Hewitt 49, 56
   Theodore 53, 54
Bolles
   W. P. 70

Boyd
   John G. 79
   Joseph 67
Boyle
   Francis 55
   Frank P. 81
Bradley
   C. W. 45
Bray
   Charles 19
Bridge Street 14
Brinnier
   William D. 67, 82, 83, 85
   William D. Jr. 93, 94
Broadhead
   John C. 17
Broadway 25, 39, 48, 51, 52, 57-60, 63, 65, 67, 70, 72, 73, 75, 76, 79, 81, 82, 84-86, 88-94, 97
Brooks
   Frank W. 82
Brown
   Frank 53, 54
Browns Hotel 13
Bruyn
   Augustus 22
   Charles D. 22
Burhans
   Cornelius 22
Butler
   Edward R. 81
Callagne
   J. J. 67
Campbell and Dempsey 33, 49
Canfield 82
Care
   Leo 92
Carey
   Eugene B. 93
Cedar Street 33, 40, 48, 51, 57, 58, 84, 86, 89
Chamber of Commerce 84, 87
Chambers 53
Chase
   Emory A. 43
Chester Street 22
Chestnut Street 12, 13
Chipp
   Howard 82
Clarke
   Herbert A. 83
Clearwater 54, 58, 63
Clifton Avenue 92, 94, 95, 97
Clinton Avenue 32, 68, 74, 84, 86, 89, 90, 94, 97

Cloonan 63
   John T. 56
Codwise
   G. Wallace 40, 77
Cohen
   Ben 79
Colonial City division 71, 73, 74, 76, 78, 79, 81, 84, 85 87, 88
Colonial City Electric Railroad 31-33, 38-42
Colonial City Traction Company 43, 48-68, 70, 71, 86, 93
Connelly
   A. C. 88
Cook
   A. J. 80
Cornell
   Thomas 12, 16, 18, 23
Cornell building 72
Cornell Steamboat Company 53
Cornell Street 33, 48, 49, 52
Cornell Towing Company 72
Costello 51
Coykendall
   George 59
   Samuel D. 14, 19, 29, 32, 41, 48, 50, 52, 57-63, 65, 70
Cramer
   Frank 53
   Herbert 53, 54
Crawford
   Joseph 45
Crosby
   A. H. 32
Crown Street 96
Curtis
   J. 67
Darling 49
Decker
   Martin S. 82, 83
Dederick Street 51, 54, 59, 67, 84
Deegan 76, 77
DeGarmo 91, 92
   William H. 23
Delaware Avenue 41, 51, 61, 73, 75, 84, 86, 92, 97
Dempsey
   E. J. 91, 94, 97
DeWitt
   Henry R. 82
   J. 79
Deyo
   C. W. 32
   Daniel B. 92

Diamond trucks 55, 67
Dimmick
    Samuel P. 19
Division Street 12, 15-17, 20
Donahue
    Floyd 81
Downs Street 86
Dressell
    Fred M. 92
DuMond 62
Dumont 18
Eagle Hotel 25
East Chester Street 95, 97
East Strand 85, 88
East Union Street 60, 71, 92
Eckert 54
    John W. 82
Esopus Creek 9, 19
Every
    Merritt 88
Fain
    John J. 81
Fair Street 15, 21, 24, 25, 31, 56, 72, 84, 87, 94, 97
Ferry Street 12, 21, 24, 31, 34, 53, 59, 64, 72, 75, 78, 94, 97
ferryboat
    Lark 24
Fiero
    J. N. 54
First National Bank of Rondout 12
Flannery
    Walter 75, 76, 81
Flatbush Avenue 86
Flemming
    H. H. 97
Flynn
    Patrick J. 19, 23
Foxhall Avenue 95
Franklin Street 86
Frescoln
    Samuel W. 65
Frescoln Company 67
Gaasbeck
    P. M. 14
Garden Street 12, 17, 95
General Electric Company 34, 35, 40, 50, 51
Gillespie
    W. Scott 32
Goodwin
    Wendell 38, 39, 49, 50, 54
Grand Street 33
Green Street 13, 25
Grimm
    John 79
Grogan
    William H. 96

Gross' Mill 52, 55
Haines 92
Hale
    Wilbur 22
Hales
    Joseph 78
Hannon
    Timothy J. 81
Hasbrouck
    Abram 56, 71
    Conrad E. 56
    Gilbert D. B. 56-59, 63
    Guilford 56
    J. DePuy 82
    James 32
    Jansen 12
    Jonathon H. 12
Hasbrouck Avenue 32, 33, 41, 48, 51, 53, 55, 73, 76, 84, 86, 89, 90, 94, 95, 97
Hauser
    Richard 75
Hayes
    William M. 23
Healey
    Daniel 79
Heldrone
    Charles 77
Henry Street 32, 89, 90, 97
Hermance
    Lewis N. 12
Herrick
    D. Cady 41, 42, 52, 54
Higginsville 19, 22, 29
Highland Avenue 95, 97
Hill 82, 84
Hilton
    Charles M. 45
Holmes
    Hiram 70
Holt
    William T. 23
Hood 61, 62
Hotel Eichler 67
Houg
    Walter M. 43
Huddler
    Alfred 39, 40
Hudson River Telephone Company 74
Hull
    John 92
Humphrey
    Horace 22
Hussey
    John 19
Hutton
    George 56
    William 33, 56

Irvin 88
Irwin
    John F. 62
Jackson and Sharpe Company 67
Jacob's Valley 65
Jenkins
    James 82, 88
Jewell Betty Company 50
John Street 28, 74
Jones
    J. H. 45
Joyce
    Martin 81
Keator
    Chauncey 19
Keiffer
    Jona 13
Kelly
    E. a. 80
Kennedy
    David 32
Kennyey
    John A. 70
Kingston and Rondout Horse Railroad Company 12, 15, 18, 32, 33
Kingston City division 71, 74, 76, 79, 81, 84-88
Kingston City Electric Railroad Company 31, 32-34, 38-40, 43, 48, 50-61, 63-68, 70, 71, 93
Kingston City Hospital 53, 79
Kingston City Transportation Company 86, 89-98
Kingston Consolidated Railroad Company 71, 73, 75, 7782, 84-95, 97
Kingston Gas & Electric Company 82
Kingston Point 57, 59, 64, 71, 75, 85, 86, 88, 95, 97
Kingston Point Park 70, 80
Kingston Taxpayer's Association 85, 90
Kingston-Rhinecliff ferry 71
Klein
    Harry 55
Klingberg
    Wilgott 53, 54, 57, 62
Klingberg & Clark 48
Kostocki
    Wasil 79
Kraft
    John E. 50-52, 54, 56, 60
Kuehn 81
Layghran
    E. H. 32

Lawrence
   E. G. 32
Layng
   J. D. 49
Learned
   Wiliam L. 60
Ledlie
   Charles H. 57
Lemister 76, 77
Leudthe
   Frederick 68
Ley
   Fred T. 77, 94
Linderman Avenue 32, 40, 57, 78, 86
Lindsley
   James G. 18
Link
   Charles 53
Linson
   John J. 42
Litus
   Mike 79
Long Island Railroad 45
Longyear
   Manasseh 19, 21
Lounsberry
   William 19, 22
Ludlum
   Catherine 22
Lusk
   Frank 54
Madden
   Michael J. 12, 19
Maiden Lane 96
Main Street 32, 72, 84, 87, 94, 97
Manhayyan Trust Company of New York 77
Mansfield
   John 41
Mansion House 34, 76
Marchlor 76
Marius Street 71, 78, 82, 89
Masten
   Peter 22
McAndrews
   Susie 76
McCullough 74
McNalty
   John 25
Measter
   Peter 60
Melieuzuk
   Denko 79
Mellert
   William 55
Mercantile Trust Company 39, 55, 56
Merritt

Chester 33
   F. C. 90
   James O. 22
Mill Street 76
Miller
   H. J. 70
Miner
   Charles 22
Molyneaux 91
Moore
   Joseph T. 80
More
   Sarah 22
   William C. 12
Mowell
   John J. 76
Mulligan
   Kate 53
Munn 53
Murphy 53
   Charles 72
   Dick 72
Muray 62
   B. J. 67
Murray Street   53, 86, 97
Music Hall 16, 24
Myers 68
   Herbert 97
National Bank of Rondout 57
Near
   Andrew 22
New Kirk Avenue 18
New York Central 91
New York, Kingston and Syracuse Railroad 17, 19
Newark Lime & Cement Company 41, 75
Newcomb
   Alva S. 41, 42, 54, 59
Noone
   Luke 22
North Front Street 13, 17, 19, 28, 31, 32, 35, 71, 79, 82, 86-89, 94, 96, 97
North Street 60, 61, 92
Norton
   James 33, 53, 70
Norwood 53
O'Hara
   John J. 42
O'Neill Street 32
O'Reillys 13
Osborne 22
Osterhoudt
   Mrs. John 75, 76
Ostrander
   Thomas P. 53
Paige 89
Parker 41, 49, 50, 54, 56-59, 63

Parsons 85
Payne
   B. W. 35
Payne-Corliss 34-36
Peckham trucks 43, 50, 55
Pennsylvania Railroad 45
Pennsylvania Steel Company 34, 77
Perrine
   Oliver A. 60
Pitts
   Henry H. 32
Powell
   Floyd M. 88
Powell dock 12, 13
Powelson
   N. C. 32, 40, 41, 48
Powers 60
Powler
   A. Ray 92, 93
Preston
   Charles M. 56, 57, 59, 60, 70
   Otis M. 56
Prince Street 48, 51, 54, 57, 58, 67, 71, 84, 86, 89, 95
Public Service Commission 81, 82, 84-91, 95, 96, 98
Pullman Company 34, 43, 50, 55, 61, 68
Railroad Avenue 458, 51, 55, 57, 59, 60, 67
Reed and McKibben 39, 41, 56
Reel
   C. Gordon 71, 75, 78
Rhinecliff ferry 89, 93
Rider
   Jacob 13, 16
Ritch
   E. J. 92
Robinson 45
Roe
   Chester B. 51, 67, 75, 79, 81
Rondout and Oswego Railroad 16, 17, 63
Rondout Creek 9, 75, 78
Rondout Social Mannerchor 67
Roosa
   Fred 78
   Joy 97
Rosa
   Hyman 25
Roy
   Herbert F. 94
Russell
   Pierce 94
   Wiliam F. 56, 59
Sahler
   Artemas 19, 23
Sampson's Opera Hopuse 25

Samson
    Henry A. 12
Sansons
    J. B. S. 18
Schepmoes 32
Schermerhorn 77
Schleede
    Charles 51
Schoonmaker
    Hiram 19
Schutt
    Sadie 76
Seifferth
    Mrs. James 52
Shader
    Chris 25
Sharpe
    S. B. 57
Short
    Jefferson 81
Sleight
    George S. 56
Smith
    George T. 32
Smith Avenue 33, 49, 51
Snyder
    Henry D. H. 12
    Robert A. 42
Soop
    H. C. 41
St. James Street 24, 31, 39, 84, 97
St. Joseph's Church 96
St. Joseph's Parachial School 96
St. Louis Car Company 43, 55, 57
St. Mary's Church 53, 72
Stafford
    C. B. 74
Staple's mill 76
State of New York Bank 20
steamer
    A. B Valentine 18
    James Madison 13
    James W, Baldwin 18, 20, 22, 24
    Marshall 18
    Mary Powell 24, 25, 28
    Thomas Cornell 18, 20
Stelle
    Edward T. 32
Stephan Street 92, 95
Stephanson
    John 18
Stern

A. A. 53, 76
Stewart
    Charles 56
Stony Clove Railroad 34
Strand 31-33, 41, 48, 57, 59-61, 64, 76, 78, 84, 86, 89, 90, 94. 95, 97
Sudheimer
    Fred W. 79
Sullivan
    Michael 54
Swalbach 13
Sweet
    Elnathan 60
Swift
    Frederick 38, 39, 49, 50, 54
Sykes
    Lorenzo A. 12
T rail 73-75, 77, 78
Tammany 60
Taylor
    William B. 71
Taylor Street 14
TeBow
    G. Burton 77-83, 85-88, 92-94, 96
Terwilliger
    A. B. 25
Thomas Street 48, 51, 52, 55, 67, 70, 84, 88
Thompson and Houston 34
Tremper Avenue 32
Trolley Museum of New York 98
Tubby
    James G. 32
tug
    Washburn 75
Turck's Mill 64
Tuthill
    J. H. 13
Ulster & Delaware Railroad 17, 41, 45, 48, 49, 51-53, 59-64, 70, 75, 78
Union Avenue 12, 15, 18, 22-25, 31-34
Union Plank Road Company 12
Vallette
    George 38
Valsh 53
Van Buren
    James 21
Van Gassbeck

C. H. 19
Van Leuven
    Isaac 41
Van Nostrand
    Elias T. 12, 19, 23
Van Etten
    Joseph 78
VanHoovenbergh 53
VanVoorhis 88
Vaughan
    W. W. 35
Wall Street 25, 28, 32, 71, 84, 87-89
Wallkill Vallet Railroad 19
Wallkill Vallet station 21
Walradt
    Arthur E. 49, 50, 53, 54
Washington Avenue 17, 32, 40, 68, 78, 79, 82, 83, 86, 89, 93, 94, 97
Waterbury
    John I. 56, 59, 70
Webster
    Grover 79
Weiber 62, 63
Wells
    William H. 12
West Shore depot 32, 48, 67
West Shire Railroad 28, 32-34, 41-43, 45, 48, 49, 51, 52, 57-60, 65, 67, 70, 76, 79, 81, 82, 86, 90, 91
Westbrook 54
    F. L. 42
    S. S. 23
    T. B. 56
Whittaker
    George R. 92
Wilson
    Robert 32
Winne
    A. F. 32
    Benjamin J. 19
    Cornelius C. 19
    Davis 19, 23
    Henry W. 16-24, 32
    Howard C. 87-89, 96
    William 19
Woolsey
    C. A. 51
Yellow Coach Company 88, 90
Young
    H. G. 49